The Soul's Inner Statues

KAYE BOESME

AIGLETOS PRESS

2023

ISBN 978-1-7357406-2-1

This book was published by the author under Aigletos Press.
Contact information is available at kayeboesme.com

TO APOLLON AND ALETHEIA,
WITH LOVE AND GRATITUDE

Contents

What Is This Book?

The Soul's Inner Statues is a free online resource for anyone who wants to learn how to pray to Gods, available at
https://kayeofswords.github.io/soulsinnerstatues
in EPUB, PDF, and MOBI files for anyone who wants to read it. You don't have to sign up for a mailing list or give up any of your information, either — just read it in your browser or download it. There's even a copy of the formatted print book hanging out in this book's GitHub repository.

You are previewing or reading a print copy that was produced *at cost*, meaning that you (or the original buyer of this book) only paid for the material and distribution cost.

If you would like to pay what you think this book is worth, please donate to a charity — your choice. Two excellent examples are Doctors Without Borders (Medicins Sans Frontières) and Survival International.

Thank you for picking up this book, and let's get started.

Chapter 1

Introduction

Welcome to this book about starting a prayer practice, an awakening of the soul's inner statues and icons to bring the Gods into one's life. Its title is a reference to a speech in Plato's *Symposium*, one of many dialogues that Plato wrote starring his deceased teacher, Socrates. In that dramatic work, a lapsed student — Alcibiades, well-known in the ancient world for straying from the path of self-discovery and love of wisdom for a disastrous career in politics — bursts into a drinking party where each attendee has been giving a speech on Eros. He describes Socrates as the statue of a woodland spirit (a satyr), hollow and filled with small icons of Gods. Socrates drives Alcibiades to evaluate his actions and attempt at being better, a jolt every time they encounter each other. Alcibiades is acutely aware that he can be so much more despite his powerlessness in the face of the strong vices and emotions that throw him into bad situations.

Like Alcibiades, we are all divided into many pieces, from work to family to society, our awareness cast about from thing to thing like a tiny vessel trying not to capsize on a tumultuous ocean. We struggle to know *where* we are, let alone *who* we are; forgetting our intrinsic wholeness, we seek to be whole. Coming to see the statues hidden within ourselves and the divine beings they represent — and anchoring ourselves to these divine ones in the quest to flourish as human beings — can go a long way to securing our inner calm, even in the face of grueling challenges, calamities, or the daily grind of work and life. Unlike Alcibiades, whose life story had long been set by the time Plato started writing the *Symposium*, we each still have opportunities to grow and change for the better in this lifetime.

The Soul's Inner Statues aims at being a small guidebook: a collection of tips and practices that can withstand the ocean's sprays of water and stinging salt. It is intended to be a systemic synthesis useful to those of us in current times, especially we who live in cultural melting pots like the United States, as we ponder what allures us about the dazzling statues of Gods and the strange stories hidden beneath the husk of commercialization and popular entertainment.

Finally, it is a hymn, both to the Gods and the underlying unity of all things that cannot be named, let alone conceived — to the ones whose images are nestled within our souls like jewels awaiting discovery and reunion with our everyday selves. "All things are full of Gods," the ancient Greek statesman Thales once said. Iamblichus, a Syrian Platonic philosopher writing in the early common era, wrote that acknowledging that the Gods exist is "not the right way to put it"; he continued that "an innate knowledge about the gods is coexistent with our nature, and is superior to all judgment and choice, reasoning and proof" and "[t]his knowledge is united from the outset with its own cause and exists in tandem with the essential striving of the soul towards the Good" (Iamblichus, 2003). Unpacking what Iamblichus said — the assumptions we may make on first reading it, the necessity of casting off misguided beliefs, and the joyous reality that unfolds as we open ourselves to the constellations of statues and the worlds within ourselves — can guide us to the inner calm of correct opinion and to the threshold of a fulfilling spiritual practice.

1.1 The Basics

This is a book about honoring Gods, and it is designed to be a practical work grounded in theory. While writing it, I had in mind an individual — perhaps spiritual-but-not-religious, maybe religious-but-looking-for-more, even not religious at all — who wants a connection to something greater than themselves and who is curious about Gods writ large. This person is not planning to join a group right now, nor are they committed to a specific cultural tradition that worships Gods. Maybe they grew up in a monotheistic faith or atheism and are trying something new, or perhaps they grew up in a continuous, Gods-venerating tradition that feels out-of-sync with where they are in life right now. Maybe they are somewhere in between. This work could also be useful for anyone who is looking to refresh an existing practice, especially those struggling with work-life balance.

This primer will give you the basic frameworks and guidance that you need to get started with prayer, and it prioritizes what I believe will do that in a healthy way: small systems and small actions that, when taken together and approached mindfully, can create a sustainable engagement with the Gods. The word choice I have opted for in this book is intentionally uplifting and positive, as starting up or changing a spiritual regimen can be daunting for even the most motivated, not to mention those of us juggling intense periods at the office with our desire to meditate and light some incense every now and then. Deciding to do something about our desire for spiritual wholeness means that any reader has likely already encountered an overwhelming amount of information — some good, some out-of-context, some wrong. You may think you need to be a specific type of person to pray or that it requires building specialist knowledge when in fact most people who pray are not religious specialists — we're ordinary people. Let's embrace that.

Anyone, no matter what our background, can develop a fulfilling private spiritual practice, and that is why this primer exists. We will refer to this fulfilling practice as *ritual*, sometimes as *prayer*, and we will direct that ritual focus at the Gods.

Much as exercise is good for the body and meditation is good for the mind, revering the Gods is good for the soul. As with activities to strengthen the body and mind, establishing habitual ritual is good for its own sake — you do not need to pursue initiation, become a theologian, or seek leadership. A prayer practice is also not about magic spells or flashy Hollywood special effects. While a person may occasionally pray and ask for something specific, the primary purpose of venerating and praying to a higher power is to establish and deepen a relationship with them, a sacred dance between the devotee (in this case, you) and the holy.

Ritual practice and contemplation are simple: you set aside time, and ideally a small amount of space, to take pause and acknowledge the divine. A ritual can be something as simple as lighting an electric or flame-based candle before murmuring a prayer of gratitude for waking up to another day. It could be pouring cool water into a bowl or sharing a few sips of one's morning coffee on the way out the door. It could be taking a few grounding breaths in front of an image of a God and spending that quiet, brief meditation cultivating fondness for and a desire to live up to the God's good qualities — all before one's young kids awaken.

For the purposes of this book, the divine consists of divine persons — Gods — who are each unique individuals. Often, when the average person thinks about Gods, the term "unique" becomes a proxy for "segmented into distinct offices" like Tupperware in the fridge after a big meal prep. Commonly-used resources online, including major dictionaries, encyclopedias, and so on, will tell you that we have a God for luck, a God for love, a God for healing, you name it. It is only after plunging into worship that we learn that many of these labels are inaccurate and overly simplistic, often applied by outsiders attempting to grapple with a system that is as dazzling and varied as nature itself. Every God is simply complicated, and as described by polytheistic philosophers and theologians, each of them is a boundary-less, unique window on the universe. Completely simple, each is an inner sanctum, a God who proceeds forth from that absolute unity. I pray to Apollon, for example, whose offices ultimately express that this God's perspective is one related to harmony. The entire universe can be viewed through that lens, and the God can encompass everything. A devotee of another God may say the same thing about the one they follow, and our perspectives can coexist in mutual acknowledgment because we have the same foundational many-Gods outlook on the world. A devotee of Oðinn, for example, is focused on a God who shares many divination attributes with Apollon, and indeed is also connected to poetry, but they have very different contexts for their behavior. They are different *individuals*.

The Gods flow forth with abundance. Like floodwaters bringing life to a desert, they give rise to intermediary spirits whose identities are often preserved in folklore, folk practices, and habitual rituals. Beyond that, the dizzyingly complex interpolation of a myriad Gods into the receptive beauty of matter causes everything around us. Coming into harmony with the Gods, as Iamblichus taught, is the foundation of human happiness. This connection is something that cannot be taken away from any of us because it is innate. Like the image of Socrates as an artisanal sculpture filled with Gods' statues, each of us *is* a unique window on divine reality. This uniqueness can be our anchor even as it emphasizes that we will each develop our perspective and connection differently. We can adapt how we live our lives through ritual, contemplation, and mindfully tuning into the seasons of the year and our lives. Becoming conscious of our connection to the Gods is a lifelong process, a dance around that anchor. Regular practice enriches our awareness of it no matter how much the winds howl when we check the news.

Despite calling a spiritual practice *simple,* I know that it can be very daunting to start one. Speaking as an American, many of us are taught that spiritual practice is something you start by paying money to attend a yoga class in a chic studio or filling a seat in a church beside other people who may or may not actually want to be there. Additionally, we think we each must declare ourselves to *be something,* and we pile label after label upon ourselves, mistaking the labels for a sense of meaning and belonging.

We may even feel anxious about praying at all: here, doing a prayer or small ritual every day can be viewed as strange or over-the-top because most spiritual communities that do that are not very visible in the United States. However, taking time for daily spiritual practice and development is far from uncommon in spiritual and religious traditions. Zen practitioners, if they want to move from casual to proficient, are expected to do at least two hours of zazen practice each day as a *layperson* (Moore, 2020:note 16). Muslims pray five times each day, and it is expected of everyone who is capable of it. In Shinto, those who keep kamidana (a type of household shrine for Kami, a word that describes a wide range of spiritual beings) give offerings daily, at least aspirationally (Chart, 2020).

In this broader context, taking two to ten minutes a day to devote to one's spiritual practice is achievable to most people.

This primer will take that statement — again, *two to ten*

minutes is achievable — and provide guidance to *make* it achievable.

1.2   Recommended Supplies

Each of these chapters contains small exercises designed to connect you to an aspect of the topic under investigation. Sometimes, you will benefit from using ritual objects. I recommend having a small bowl on hand, a vessel (like a jar) that contains water, and a slip of paper with the God's name written on it. If you can clear off a part of one shelf, that is ideal. If not, just use a clean surface and store your prayer materials in a clean box when you're not using them.

Sometimes, no matter what, we run into challenges setting aside space. If you live in a college town, May is a great time to find tables and shelves cheaply (or for free), as students are leaving, and many of them are on tight move-out deadlines. FreeCycle and other no-buy groups are other options. If this is not possible, or if you are waiting for the right time to find a place for your shrine, make space on your floor or wall that you can dedicate to the Gods. I found an online article about young South Asians coming to the United States and how they set up their sacred areas to be particularly inspiring for thinking about what one can do with limited space (Upadhyaya, 2021). IKEA recently came out with a cutting board with legs. It is inexpensive and is perfect for elevating an offering space ever-so-slightly, whether you are placing it on the ground or on part of a table or desk.[1]

---

[1]Specialized furniture for religious worship exists, often "altar"/shrine

If you are unable to establish a permanent shrine space, create a folder on your smartphone with images of the hearth deities and divinities of interest to you. Turn on the phone feature that keeps the phone screen on when you're looking at it. Put the phone on a stand on a clean surface, full-screen the image after going into Airplane Mode and hitting Do Not Disturb on your phone, and offer prayers in front of the image.

You can, of course, be more elaborate. Once we get going with the exercises, you will have opportunities to offer items like incense. When we move from talking about many Gods in the generic to actually choosing which God(s) to honor, you may want to purchase icons of those Gods from Etsy or Redbubble or another online market, but don't feel pressured to do that immediately — taking a few months to a year to make a decision about them gives you time to solidify your practice first.

This book is open access for a reason: I am aware that we have a variety of economic situations. Cultivating your inner light — and connecting to the Gods — is something that is accessible no matter how simple your prayer space is. A set of small bowls and a pitcher for pouring will likely cost $3-5 at Goodwill; used sauce jars will cost you nothing more than

---

furniture. Many of these items are designed to be placed on tables or storage consoles within the home, and others are like cabinets. If you decide to eventually invest in something like that, I recommend choosing furniture items that do not show much out-of-context religious symbolism on them unless you worship someone for whom that symbolic register is appropriate. A plain Butsudan is a closed hutch box that is great for people with allergies, and a home mandir piece may work, but refrain from repurposing a kamidana — those are *highly* specific to kami. Bookshelves, console tables, and secretary's desks are other options. Just make sure that if you are lighting candles, the piece you choose does not have a shelf above the candle. That is a fire risk.

the time spent cleaning them out.

Many people end up engaging in spiritual consumerism, and they fill their prayer spaces up with material items to make themselves feel more spiritual. Everything you put in this space is a tool or a vessel to help you connect to God(s). Some parts of these spaces — particularly the images of Gods — are extremely sacred. If a fire or other disaster came, how many of these precious images could we put in our go bags? Probably not many. Be reasonable about your space and ask yourself questions about ergonomics, durability, and maintenance whenever you consider adding an icon. The same goes for furniture.

1.3   Starting Prayer

Let's take a quick pause.

Be in a space where you will not be disturbed for two minutes. (It's OK if this is your car, but the bathroom is not appropriate.) Close your eyes and take a few deep breaths. Silently count to four while breathing in and four while breathing out.

After a few cycles of breath, hold out your hands, with bent elbows, palms up. Your palms may either be together or apart.

At this point, you may either pray from the heart or use the words I am providing below. It is okay to open your eyes unless that is distracting for you.

> I honor and acknowledge the Gods I know, the
> Gods I do not know, and the good divinities willing
> to guide me. Please grant me what I need, and as

I embark on a new beginning to study how best to approach you, may the actions I undertake guide me serendipitously to the place where I can be steady, happy, and truly free.

1.4 Dedication

As one seeker of truth to another, I hope that the words in this book will be useful to your own voyage through life.

I will end the introduction with part of a prayer that I give every morning:

Please, Apollon, let me find the still heart of truth at the core of all things. Please cultivate within me skill — in my poetry, in my prose, and in all of my actions, let all that I do flow forth from you.

I will add to this a prayer to the Goddess Aletheia:

May you, Aletheia, guide the reader towards truth and grant them a sip from your compassionate, abiding nectar, and may my words in this open access book be good enough to give them what they need for their journey.

This book is dedicated to Apollon and Aletheia.

Chapter 2

Foundations

This chapter is called *Foundations* because we will dive a bit deeper into thinking about Gods — after all, they are the bedrock of everything in this book. It is also titled *Foundations* because the main practice at the end of the chapter involves the cleared-off section of shelf and small bowl from the end of the introduction.

We will look at what Gods actually are, and we will use Plato's *Laws* to unpack some common pitfalls that happen when we think about them — mindsets that most of us may have slipped into at some point or other in our lives. We will then walk through the foundations of contemplative practices, rituals, and household observances. Finally, you will have an opportunity to do some brief veneration on your own. I encourage you to go through this chapter at your own pace and to take notes.

The advice in this book is *advice* — as long as you keep the fundamental point of respect towards the Gods in mind, you will be fine. You also have the opportunity to answer questions that I will occasionally ask. They are designed to open you up to possibilities and to brainstorm ways to apply what is under discussion to your life.

One option for you when encountering these questions — or, indeed, at any point at all in your reading — is to write, either in a journal or on your phone. However, if you are a busy parent, beholden to one or more demanding jobs with no work-life balance, or writing is just not accessible right now, that's okay — modify as needed. Real life is not a stylized "what I do in a day" video, and it is definitely not a curated social media photograph. Think about these questions while you are in the shower, during your commute, or when completing tasks that don't require a heavy cognitive load, like folding laundry. If something comes up that you want to keep hold of for later, use a note-taking app on your phone or create a draft email that you will send to yourself.

2.1   What Is a God, Anyway?

In the introduction, I quoted from two philosophers who were operating in a similar cultural context to each other. Thales, a Greek philosopher who was active before Socrates' lifetime (and is thus called a "Pre-Socratic"), said that the world is full of Gods; Iamblichus, a Syrian fluent in both his native culture and Greek culture of the late third century of our common era, described a God's existence as a given, but strangely so.

Not once did I bring up the predominant understanding of the word *God* in current times, which is often regarded as a *specific* someone — a singular omnipotent, omnipresent, omniscient being who is tied to the initiatory rites of revealed religions, a being only accessible when someone adheres to the correct holy book and doctrines. Sometimes in spiritual circles, people pray to the Source, Spirit, or the One as a way of being "generic" and "accessible," referring to a single God while trying to avoid salvific baggage and bad memories. My reluctance to discuss this broader cultural material is partly related to my own background — my outlook on the Gods is Platonizing, which means that I do not believe that the first principle is capable of being described in that way. Even before my outlook was Platonizing, I grew up Neopagan, and my perspective on the Gods has always been very positive. I admit that I had significant misgivings about the theology I was first taught in the late 90s and early 00s: We collapsed Gods into one God and Goddess, ultimately Spirit, which never felt right. I hungered for more weighty theology, and that is what led me to Plato. This book is grounded in my perspective (although it's designed to be accessible and useful to people who do *not* identify as Platonists or Platonizing). My second reason for *not* bringing it up in the introduction was that doing so would set an inappropriate tone for this work — this work is not a defense of Gods, but in praise of them. My third reason is that I want to push back against the totalizing understanding of words like *god, deity,* or *divinity.* Many of us assume what these words mean based on tacit things we learned as children, not on anything systematic.

God is used as a class term for a wide range of divine persons, sometimes accurately, sometimes imprecisely. Often, the term is used when translating indigenous terms for divine beings. The word *spirit* is used just as often. The Shinto term *Kami*, for example, describes a range of beings, many of them more reminiscent of divinities like nymphs, river spirits and Gods of place, or house wights. The words *theos* and *daimon* in Greek are equally problematic. A daimon is an intermediary spirit that carries out specific functions, but sometimes, a God is called a daimon in surviving writings from Ancient Greece! River divinities are usually referred to with *theos*, but are they a *theos* in the same way the Goddess Athene is? Are planetary Gods similar to other Gods even though most planetary bodies will perish when their stars go nova, or are they more like extremely long-lived nature spirits? Which, if any, beings from another language receive the term "God"? "Spirit"? "Wight"?

Ultimately, the answers to those questions depend on the biases of who is translating and if they have a specific set of beings in mind when they choose a word. This is one reason why Wikipedia is often not as good as going to a religious organization's website (or, for decentralized religions, a few sites put together by different practitioners, ideally ones who are not in the same communication bubbles) to learn what its adherents believe. One helpful resource for comparative theology, including information about terminology and how cultures' diverse views on what deities are and how to worship them inform their cosmologies, is Edward Butler's *The Way of the Gods: Polytheism(s) Around the World*, based on a course he taught in 2021 (Butler, 2022).

Theological and philosophical exercises can help us narrow down what these categories mean. In Platonism, my theological framework, these elastic terms have been refined into four classes: gods, angels, daimons, and heroes. The final three classes are sometimes grouped under "daimons." Each of the daimonic classes has less contact with the ultimate divine reality and more contact with variability and change. Divinities of the natural world and household inhabit the spaces "closest" to us. You and I are located at the level just below heroes — we are souls that incarnate in material bodies according to a long, regular cycle; a small sliver of us is permanent and godlike like the beings closer to godhood than us, and that is what we want to cultivate as *I* in a spiritual practice. Other philosophical schools, like Yogic philosophy, Stoicism, or Daoist philosophy, have different takes on this. Generally speaking, though, we are all trying to become as godlike as possible, to pull from Plato's *Theaetetus* (176a-b).

The *strict* definition of God I will take — and the one I mean when I discuss our inner core of happiness and the statues within us — are those individual divine persons who ground the entirety of reality. They slip and slide into one another, boundary-free because they preexist both limit and unlimitedness. They are the ones whom we ultimately uncover in our practices. What is visible in breathtaking photographs from a space telescope or witnessed in the powerful fury of the world around us, or even the small actions of our daily lives, are all ultimately grounded in *their* astonishing foundation.

It is no wonder that Iamblichus wrote that "an innate knowledge about the gods is coexistent with our nature" and that they just *are*, but strangely so. All of the beings following from the Gods are nourished by their divinity, including the material world.

Most of the time, I will refer to other categories of divine beings as spirits, daimons, or divinities. I will also occasionally refer to ancestors. There may even be a triad of *Gods, spirits/daimon(e)s, and ancestors* in some of these materials, although ancestor worship is not the primary focus of this book. The spellings of *daimones* and *daimons* are interchangeable and simply note differences in how people shift the term from Ancient Greek to English during transliteration and adaptation.

- What are the definitions you have heard for the term *God*? How do they differ from what I have said?

- Look up the divine beings in three distinctly different traditions. What are the similarities? Differences? How well does the term *God* fit what you see?

2.2 Mindset Lessons from Plato

One passage from Plato's *Laws* can ground our understanding of the Gods even more. Plato's *Laws* is a long city-soul analogy that describes how parts of the soul function in an embodied context, and it was questionably complete when Plato died — some parts of it seem rushed, and some analogies that are stridently hammered through by the speakers in later books are not as deftly scaffolded into earlier sections of the *Laws* as they are in Plato's other works, especially when compared to the care he took in his other long city-soul analogy, the *Republic*. The *Laws* is said to have still been "on the wax" when he died, meaning that it had not been transferred to a more lasting medium like his finished pieces. In the Platonic tradition, Plato's writings are approached somewhat like puzzles or myths to be interpreted by someone with skill, usually after years of preparation. A successful interpretation or commentary is inspired by the Muses and other Gods, identifying the signatures of truth within the words. Commentaries can be very different from one another while still communicating the same truth. It is the inspiration that matters, which leads to a successful weaving of Platonic concepts as an interpreter works through each piece's components. These facts about how the *Laws* was transmitted make it a particularly tricky text to interpret.

Plato's works (apart from his letters) take the form of dialogues — dramatic vignettes in which speakers encounter one another and ask questions, Socrates often one of the primary interlocutors. The *Laws* does not include Socrates as a character, but an unidentified old man called the Athenian Stranger, who is doing a pilgrimage hike with two other elderly men. Like the *Republic*, it is long and broken up into many sections. Book 10 of the *Laws* contains a conversation on atheism and piety, and most followers of Plato will, at some point, work this section of the *Laws* into a commentary, treatise, lecture, blog post, or social media thread to illustrate what proper and respectful conduct towards the Gods actually means. Now is the perfect opportunity for us to take a look at it.

The Athenian Stranger says:

> People [commit offenses] in one of three frames
> of mind: either lacking the belief [in the Gods]
> I mentioned; or second, believing that there *are*

gods, but that they care nothing for human beings; or third, that they are easily won over by inducements in the form of sacrifice and prayer. (Plato, 2016:885b)

In Platonism, an embodied rational soul has three parts: our thinking part, which can connect to the Gods and which survives death, and an irrational soul divided in two, the emotional and appetitive parts. The irrational soul perishes because our feelings and appetites are contingent on our specific embodiment (although depending on the person one asks, some aspects of the irrational soul can persist across several lifetimes; additionally, which traits are intrinsic to a partial soul and which ones depend on the body are still a lively area of debate). Our consciousness, and our self, is lasting. The three types of atheism correspond roughly to the three parts of the soul. A lack of belief in Gods is an intellectual atheism. Believing the Gods do not care or influence us is an atheism of care, an alienation from our own emotionality. Believing they can be swayed by offerings is an atheism of appetite. Proper piety requires unlearning these three traps so we can get out of our own way.

In the *Laws*, the Athenian Stranger discusses the lack of belief in Gods by referencing the planetary bodies and other types of natural phenomena as a way to jolt someone into reverence. Writing in 2022, as someone with a love of modern astronomy, it was dissatisfying for me at first to read the discussion. At face value, his argument relies on outmoded ways of looking at the cosmos. We do not believe that the Earth is at the center — the planets orbit the Sun, and the

Sun orbits the center of the Milky Way, which inhabits a local group of galaxies that is in a region of galaxies called the Virgo Supercluster. Our robots have been to the surface of Mars, and they probe the secrets of Venus. We may even have dedicated scientific probes orbiting Europa soon. Of course, in Late Antiquity, it was recognized by many religious people that the planets and the Gods were not the same. Each of the Gods is connected to *every planet*, and how we assign Gods to parts of the cosmos has a significant cultural component — it's based on a God's "conversation" with a culture as the culture and the God get to know one another, usually via bursts of inspiration and serendipity mixed with logical insights. Ishtar is associated with the planet Venus because that association expresses something about the Goddess and about the cultures who call that planet hers.

What bothered me is rooted in a common problem among many of us in the United States — our culturally-specific baggage. The dominant form of religion here has a strong anti-science contingent. When we think about Gods, especially in America, we are living in the shadow of the way Christian religious rhetoric operates in the public sphere. We are living in the wake of that religion's Great Awakenings, most recently in the charismatic and evangelical waves of the mid-20th century with their prosperity gospel, cultivated distrust of science, and weaponized piety. While some of the televangelists, like Jim Bakker, have diminished cultural relevance due to scandals and/or jail time, this remains a very vocal American subculture, and some of its ideas diffuse into the broader culture without us realizing it. For example, we are encouraged to view jobs as *callings*, a jargon word from Christianity for divine service, to prevent burnout when work gets rough. Often, our reluctance to engage with the divine is based on an inner fear that we will end up exactly like those toxic people, organizations, and cultural zeitgeists, or we are driven by the desire for social approval to not investigate Gods at all because "there are many Gods" is not a common position for someone to have in the United States right now, and we feel shame about our impulse to do so.

I was born in the late 1980s and experienced American public schooling in the 1990s and early 2000s. When I was in 9th grade, our biology teacher told the class — a rural school filled with students who had been taught that evolution was hubristic sin against their sacred texts — that he didn't believe in evolution, but he was obligated to teach it, and we had better fill out the state exams in a way that the graders of the exams liked so our school could continue to get funding. I had been taught a non-Christian form of intelligent design by my parents — the divine created the cosmos, but science describes how the cosmos actually operates. In 2001, intelligent design was *also* a hubristic sin to many Christians. It wasn't until a few years later that it became a tool for ultra-conservative Christians to sneak Biblical creationism into school curricula. For a few years, it was very possible to believe in a divine origin for the cosmos *and* to love and appreciate science, and to do so publicly in intellectual circles, without anyone caring.

I choose to read Plato's Athenian Stranger as trying to jolt people into contextualizing their feelings of awe at the natural world. A deep, connected feeling in prayer is very similar to the feeling one gets when seeing the night sky in a place with very little light pollution or when we witness sunlight pierce through summer foliage in a breathtaking way. When it rains, I sometimes think of the diamond rain on Neptune, Uranus, and (possibly) Jupiter and fall into silence — it is that smallness, that sense of being tuned into what is common between the worlds, that makes me feel connected to the cosmos and in awe of all that is. The same patterns exist everywhere. Nothing is exotic, and the Gods and daimons fill everything, even the space between celestial bodies.

Let's look at the Iamblichus I quoted in the introduction again. Conceding the Gods' existence is "not the right way to put it" — but why? He continues with "an innate knowledge about the gods is coexistent with our nature, and is superior to all judgment and choice, reasoning and proof" and "[t]his knowledge is united from the outset with its own cause and exists in tandem with the essential striving of the soul towards the Good" (Iamblichus, 2003: I.3) — but how? And do all of us really feel that way, deep down? If we become quiet, if we progress from the turbulence of our daily lives to rest in that stillness, will knowledge of Gods just flow forth? Yes — in the quiet of sublime moments, when our defenses slip, we know that inner steadiness and connection to them.

The Gods are not their myths, and they crown the totality of the cosmos, not just Earth. They are the preface to existence, and what they have lain down forms the scaffolding of everything we see in the universe. The universe itself is a Goddess. She expresses her order in a beautiful array of mathematical brilliance, in both the mundane everyday of our lives and the half-grasped dreams of theoretical physicists. Looking to a physical object like the Moon or a planet (or contemplating a story about diamond expolanets) anchors us in a distant, still-corporeal thing — unless we use that knowledge of other worlds to jostle ourselves out of our subjective experience. It is that intellectual flight that we want to cultivate.

Beyond that discussion of how contemplating the natural world can draw us up to contemplating the Gods, the logic of belief and the Gods depends on several factors, ranging from philosophical schools' doctrines to deep, indescribable personal experiences. Proclus' *Platonic Theology*, Book I, explains how the Gods fit into the emanative system of Platonism and how they transcend existence itself, and he uses language that is most accessible to those who have already studied Platonic dialogues and doctrines (Proclus, 1995). Were this book to dive deeper into Platonic doctrines, I might answer those questions by focusing my attention on the types of divine inspiration and the way that the structure of the Gods' unfolding from ultimate unity underpins all that is, the Divided Line of the *Republic,* and what Socrates says about madness in the *Phaedrus.* I would also turn to Proclus' *Elements of Theology* and explore a few of its propositions. Similar arguments occur in Stoic, yogic, and other works using the schema of each system — if you have a school in mind and are curious about it, I encourage you to jot down notes to remember for when we get to the Lifelong Learning chapter, and indeed I recommend you do that anytime I write about how I think about ritual from a Platonic standpoint. Spiritual and philosophical schools have different names because they have different positions on these things! What these diverse schools' doctrines all come down to, though, is that looking for a "god of the gaps" or saying "god works in mysterious ways" are not correct statements.

Setting the Gods as the *base layer* of reality that gives rise to our material heterogeneity, regardless of the details of the specific philosophical and theological system, harmonizes all of existence with our unique personal experiences, or lack thereof; in each system, we are trying to reach a place where we can see both the forest and the trees without dissociating from either perspective. There are no gaps. Everything around us is produced by the Gods' activity, a direct result of *them*. Learning about the Gods may be complicated, and exploring how their beautiful unity unfolds is a daunting and frustrating task at times. We don't always agree with others on the details. What we uncover through deep thought and experience, though, is ineffable, an understanding that defies reduction into words. This is not mysterious — just challenging to communicate.

The second type of error, *believing that the Gods do not care*, comes from several roots. It is a way of cutting off our feelings and our emotional investment — insulating ourselves from everyday disappointments and coping with the seemingly random horrors that come to pass in our lives. Sometimes, we cultivate this mindset because we believe it is the best way to be realistic and logical. It is certainly true that the universe is enormous. We are each very small in comparison.

Plato's Athenian Stranger said:

> The gods are on our side — as also are the guardian

spirits — and we in turn are the property of the gods and guardian spirits. What is fatal for us is injustice, and arrogance allied to folly; our salvation is justice, and self-control allied to wisdom, and these are to be found dwelling in the living powers of the gods — though they can also be seen dwelling in us, just a bit — or something very like them. (Plato, 2016:906b)

In the system that Plato built, we are part of the organizational structure of the cosmos. We may be small, but we are each capable of developing agency and learning how to be as good and godlike as possible. Everything we see and touch, including ourselves, is part of the universe and the Gods' collaborative creation of it. Gods, intermediary spirits, and our guardian spirits look after the whole and the parts within the whole. It is not conceited for a rose in a garden to know that its caretaker is checking its roots, pruning its leaves, and ensuring it grows well.

Sometimes, it's admittedly hard to think about the whole. We are living on a small planet in a vast universe. Even considering Earth alone, the climate crisis touches each of us. Many of us live in less than perfect circumstances. We learn of new horrors near and far every day.

One challenge of the material world is that it has spatial and temporal extent, unlike the levels of reality that ground everything. The cosmos must unfold in time, and the way the pre-cosmic levels — whose components overlap and interpenetrate without spatiality or conflict — "freeze" into the material world introduces interference patterns. The evils we experience, the conflicts that devastate us, and the imperfections of the material world are all produced by this. When we incarnate, we make the best choice of life we can based on the options available to us and our disposition — and, like deciding between a tooth extraction and a root canal, sometimes having a healthy tooth is just not on the table. We can possess realistic awareness of our material surroundings while holding the Gods as good. Once embodied, we do possess some level of agency. We can make the options better or worse for the souls choosing lives on this planet in the future, including our own, through deliberate effort to tackle challenges and create the societies we want. This requires cultivating virtue and discipline, and it also requires cultivating the self-compassion that is crucial for taking care of ourselves as we strive to be better people.

Now, let's talk about appetitive atheism, or the belief we can sway the Gods with offerings. Many of us who have looked at *National Geographic* or who have taken any world history class know that offerings to Gods are a huge component of many societies. When I originally learned about Ancient Greece and Rome, for example, it was explained that the elaborate systems of offerings were used to goad the Gods into granting us favor — and this idea was backed up in plays, epics, and other written pop culture works from the ancient Mediterranean. To this day, there are people who attempt to bribe the Gods to "offset" immoral behavior, like lies and theft. Believing this is possible means believing that the Gods are *not* good or stable. It means believing that they are vulnerable to appetites. Anything that has an appetite lacks something, which means it is not complete or perfect. People like that do not possess divine favor.

This apparent paradox is most apparent when we look at myth. In myths, Gods can have very strong appetites, with good or disastrous impacts. Many of these stories are violent. The stories force us to look deeper at what the myth is actually saying about how a God impacts the world. I will only touch on this briefly here, but I recommend reading Sallust/Sallustius' "On the Gods and the World," Chapter IV (Sallust, 1793). In that chapter, Sallust discusses how myths operate and how we interpret them. He breaks down the levels of operation of myths into theological, physical, soul-oriented, and natural processes or materially-oriented. Additionally, there are "mixed" myths that operate at multiple levels simultaneously.

For anyone who has done literary criticism, the practice of mythic exegesis is very similar. For example, in one myth, Medusa is transformed and exiled by Athene after being raped by Poseidon in Athene's temple. Athene then has a champion hero, Perseus, go to the lair of Medusa to kill her and bring back the head. Athene then uses this head to adorn her body. Athene is an intellectual Goddess — philosophical and wisdom-filled, virginal and separated from generative actions like sex. In the Platonic tradition, the soul begins its journey in contact with the wisdom, beauty, truth, and love in the highest places our souls can access. At some point, we lose our stability and plunge into generation, the term for the material cosmos of "coming-to-be," and we lose access to that nourishment in the discordant fall. This descent is a necessary thing for us — our souls do it to complete the universe and bring the providence of the Gods into contact with what is always changing. However, there is a heavy price. The descent into generation is a descent into what is alien to us, a place where we can never exist without violence or pain. Poseidon is the Lord of the World of Becoming and is the ruler of generation — his violence is a symbol of how our soul experiences our alienating, violating descent. Medusa here represents the soul. She is depicted with wings, reminiscent of the metaphorical wings we lost during our descent. The serpents represent renewal, the many incarnations the soul must go through, all attached to her reasoning core. Her petrifying gaze renders every living thing around her stone, much as we all fail, in some way or other, to truly see the living beings around us. Instead, we transform them into objects and fail to see them for what they are — a monstrous disaster for both ourselves and others. Perseus, as a heroic spiritual intermediary, liberates Medusa from the body and returns the head (symbolizing the immortal part of the soul) to Athene, her proper guardian, completing the soul's cycle. Medusa becomes harmonious with the Goddess once again through directing her petrifying activity in tandem with the warlike Goddess' motions.

This interpretative analysis has several further implications that I could ponder: What does it mean to view the descent into generation as negative, given that the above interpretation includes elements of violence and loss? How do we view Medusa's older sisters, who are both *wholly* immortal in some stories, unlike the mortal Medusa? Does the presence of these sisters preserve or present problems to the interpretation? If every God is good, how do we interpret the violence of descent, as a God (Poseidon) presides over that violence?

The *Prolegomena to Platonic Philosophy* clarifies that this approach to myth is far from uncommon — in fact, it is what is necessary, as stories that have been handed down for so long (like most myths) are a chaotic bag of symbols that is frequently overwhelming for any newcomer to unpack.

> [W]hereas the poets spun their tales at random, Plato says that anyone who is going to make up a myth concerning the deity should observe certain standards that will secure his readers from error. He should know that [the] God is good and never guilty of falsehood, neither through ignorance of the truth nor from deceitfulness; and that every deity is changeless and inflexible, since they can neither change for the worse nor for the better, the one being against their nature, the other impossible; it is against [the God's] nature to change for the worse, and they cannot change for the better, being by their very essence superior to all things. This is what we mean by the propriety of his myths. Readers of myths should bear this in mind, to prevent the children from suffering harm: as soon as they plunge into the story, the good purpose should be immediately obvious from the contents, without their having to wait for the moral [...] if these rules are neglected, it will be difficult for the children to get rid of their misunderstandings. (Anonymous, 1994:β' 7.20-33)

If we think of our reactions to many of the myths when we

first hear them — an example often used by Platonists is the one of Kronos eating his children — it is clear that we are like those children mentioned in the *Prolegomena*. For many myths, deriving insight is like making lemonade. We must squeeze out the potent, bitter-sour juice of what the poets wrote and use interpretation to sweeten it into a refreshing, nourishing beverage. We are often not exposed to myths in an environment that helps us understand what they are, which harms a seeker's ability to think about the Gods in the terms Plato emphasizes here in the *Laws*. Even today, philosophers trying to help people through difficult interpretative work like this provide models for people to consult when they think about violent myths (Butler, 2019; Addey, 2000).

Contemplating and wrestling with what myths mean is something that anyone can do, even without a ritual space. It becomes easier to think through these things with time and attentiveness, and depending on which Gods one worships, one may have intricate puzzles to work through — it may take months or years of thinking about a myth before you feel like you've cracked it open. And then you discover that there is a completely new layer to the myth that you hadn't considered! The process is *rewarding*, though, for overcoming a shallow view of myths and coming to a better understanding of how appetites are not what they seem in these stories.

Establishing that the Gods are not swayed by sacrifices and that the appetites they display in myths are not to be taken at face value can (and should!) lead us to wonder about prayer. Why do we pray to the Gods, then, if they cannot be swayed and if the stories *about* them being swayed are all to be interpreted allegorically?

Proclus is fond of saying that everything prays innately, each in its own way, simply by being what it is — like a sunflower following the sun. Every one of your actions since birth has been a prayer following some God or other, whether you are aware of that or not. Earlier, I wrote that our souls are at a level below the Gods and daimons (angels, daimons proper, and heroes). In this system, we are called "rational souls" — not in the sense of Vulcans on *Star Trek*, but as a jargon term that indicates our conscious awareness and ability to achieve dialectic and intuitive reasoning, which I like to refer to as *deliberative awareness* even though the adjective *deliberative* usually means something slightly different. Our rational soul, the summit of *who* we are, is immortal, attached to worldly garments that are not immortal. We are the lowest extremity of divinity, and part of how we express our nature is by incarnating in cycles.

We spend part of the soul's cycle in close contact with the Gods, and we spend part of it down here. We are each brought down into the material world in a unique way based on our nature — to help others, perhaps, or to work through things until we regain a clear head. I will say more about this later, but we are each in the "series" of a specific God, and we thus inherit intrinsic attributes from them that impacts the choices of lives we make and what types of lives are going to be fulfilling for us.

Each of us could, in any incarnation, choose to wing it and go with the flow. Chances are, if you've picked up this book, that is not something that you want to do, but you can always close this and go live your life. Prayer — the *intentional* focus on the Gods — keeps our awareness anchored in our close, foundational contact with divinity. Physical tools we might use in prayer — the statues, the incense, the chants, whatever — support cultivating awareness and connection when used *wisely*. This is true regardless of how enormous and multi-pronged the challenges we face are. Prayer, and the spiritual impact of that intentional connection, keeps us rooted. It builds our resilience and invites us to contextualize *this specific life* — both the good and the rough times. It keeps us in contact with virtue and gives us a compassionate reality check that living lives is a process. It solidifies a growth mindset and nourishes our souls. The more mindfully we engage, the more we can adapt to what the world throws at us and bring forth good things of our own.

Additionally, the Gods still care about everything within the realm of generation. While writing about the ancient world, Andrej and Ivana Petrovic, in *Inner Purity and Pollution in Greek Religion*, quote the beliefs of Pythagoras about prayer as recorded by Diodorus Siculus:

> For he himself [Pythagoras] disclosed that wise men should pray to the gods for the good things for the benefit of the unwise, since the unwise are incapable of understanding what in life is truly good. (10.9.8) **He used to say that it was necessary in prayers to pray simply for the good things, and not to name them individually, such as for instance to pray for power, beauty, wealth, and other similar things. For often each of these things,**

when those who desired them acquire them, turning against them, totally ruins them. (A. Petrovic and I. Petrovic, 2016: 63)

Pythagoras' mindset still rings true today. Because the Gods care for us, and because they are more expansive than us, they have more secure knowledge of what is good for us. I could pray to the Gods for money, power, and fame, but if it were granted, would it actually be the best thing for me? Probably not. Studies have shown that there are hard limits on the amount of happiness and fulfillment we can achieve through material and social wealth. Many millionaires, celebrities, and rulers are absolutely miserable, moreso than the general population. A good life is a life with enough hardship to avoid complacency and to encourage learning, but with enough stability to be able to thrive. Once a person has met their basic needs, it's hard to know where that line is.

In another dialogue, the *Phaedrus*, Socrates and Phaedrus pray at the end for good things — a generic prayer that leaves the specifics of what happens up to the God, one that expresses humility about the limits of human knowledge. We do not know about the future.

You will find that many theological and philosophical systems have similar features — (often) multi-part souls, a complex relationship with mythic corpora, and a belief in the goodness of the Gods. If you have ideas about who you want to worship and which philosophical systems draw you, I encourage you to see how they handle these things. For example, traditional Nordic ideas about the soul involve many more parts than the Platonic version.

Now that we have discussed both the Gods and some common misconceptions about them, let's get into contemplative practices. As the section above may have been a lot to read through, feel free to set this primer down and stretch, take a walk, do some dishes, or whatever else helps you digest ideas.

2.3   Contemplative Practices

With or without setting aside physical space for spiritual practices, we can ground ourselves in the Gods through contemplative techniques. The title of this primer, *The Soul's Inner Statues*, likely appeals to many who have tried some form of contemplation or breathwork before, as it names the soul and evokes some kind of interior spiritual experience. You may have tried a form of meditation using the Headspace or Calm apps, pranayama techniques in a yoga class, or the practice of taking a few deep breaths before or after engaging with something difficult.

2.3.1   Foundations

If you haven't tried meditation techniques, or if your experiences have not been what you wanted, here is some good news: There are many types of contemplative techniques, not all of which require sitting down and focusing on the breath, and online instructional materials are widely available for many types of practices. Breathwork techniques, chanting guidance, and guided meditations on focal-point-based mindfulness are some of the most widespread options.

Here are a few resources to get started:

- Anusha Wijeyakumar's *Meditation with Intention: Quick and Easy Ways to Create Lasting Peace* seeks to provide useful foundations for anyone, including those who have experienced challenges when meditating. I took note of her book when I saw praise from people who have had difficulty meditating with other guidance (Wijeyakumar, 2021).

- Headspace, Calm, Healthy Minds, or another app. Both Calm and Headspace offer free trials, and Healthy Minds is free. Core features of these apps center on mindfulness meditation. You may also have access to mental wellness apps like Sanvello (which includes meditation timers) through your workplace or insurance benefits.

- For people interested in Stoicism, try out Donald Robinson's four Stoic meditation exercises[1] or the meditation app Stoa.[2]

- If you're curious about contemplative activities in Platonism, I recommend Mindy Mandell's *Discovering the Beauty of Wisdom*, which contains some contemplative techniques (Mandell, 2020).

- David Nowakowski has made a primer on techniques available on his website (Nowakowski, n.d.), and I recommend those resources, which include both Stoic and general passage contemplation meditations.[3]

To time a meditation, you can use a dedicated phone app,

---

[1] https://donaldrobertson.name/2018/03/27/four-stoic-meditation-exercises

[2] https://stoameditation.com

[3] https://davidnowakowski.net/meditation/

the timer on your watch or fitness tracker, the timer function in your clock app (with a non-jarring timer noise), or even a classic physical timer. Calm, Headspace, and other paid apps have trials that you can use if you want some guided direction when just starting out.

When starting a contemplative practice, I recommend having a plan: Know when you will do it, which tool you will use to time it, and the technique(s) you will use during the brief period.

2.3.2   Contemplating the Divine

I do daily meditation as basic mental hygiene, as do many people — ten-minute shower, ten minute-meditation, and my body and mind are ordered and ready to face the world. If we want to reach inside and open the gate to the statues within — and rest in the Gods who wait just beyond our breath — we need a divine set of focal points in addition to general mental wellness practices.

Contemplating the Divine Being

Instead of focusing on your breath, you might focus on a deity, household spirit, or ancestor you want to connect with — and don't worry if you don't know *who* quite yet.

This can be made a bit easier by using an image. If you have a smartphone, put your phone in airplane mode and make sure you have a few images saved in your photos. Create a dedicated folder so you can find them easily. My Android phone has a feature that keeps the phone on when I'm looking at it, and if yours can do similar, all you have to do is pull up one of those photos and make sure your phone can see you. You could also purchase a bookmark or postcard featuring the deity, use a printout image, or invest in artisanal divine images.[4] It works well if the deity is looking out of the image towards you because you have the illusion of eye contact.

While focusing on the deity, just breathe. You can close your eyes if you like while holding the image in your mind. Using your meditation or phone timer is useful here.

Often, when I meditate on a God, I start with prayer beads. Because I am not a crafter, I have usually purchased these beads, often from sellers on Etsy or another site for small businesses and artisans. The beads that work best for me for most contemplations are short strings with between nine and twenty beads. I have selected short phrases from content I have come across for various Gods, and I have pored through other texts to find short snippets that I want to use in some other cases. Some examples of phrases I use are:

- Οἰγνύσθω ψυχῆς βάθος ἄμβροτον· ὄμματα πάντα ἄρδην ἐκπετάννυμι ἄνω. "Let the immortal depths of my soul be opened. May all of my eyes stretch completely upward on high." This is from the *Chaldean Oracles* fragments, a slight modification of a translation by Ruth Majercik of Fragment 112 (Majercik, 2013).

- Βίος Βίος Ἀπόλλων Ἀπόλλων Ἥλιος Ἥλιος Κόσμος Κόσμος Φῶς Φῶς. "Life Life Apollon Apollon Helios Helios

---

[4]Do not go overboard on Etsy, especially if you are just starting out and don't know which deities you want to worship. That said, I have found some excellent wood bookmarks of Gods — both Norse and Hellenic. A few shops have excellent wood icons available, too.

Cosmos Cosmos Light Light." This is an inscription from the Boreikean Society, circa 300 BCE, which is used by several of us in the modern worship of Gods in completely different ways (Harland, 2013). I personally use it to get closer to Apollon, whom I associate with black holes.

- There is a chant, Οὐδὲν ἄρα οὕτως βεβαίως δεδήσεται, οὐ νόσῳ, οὐκ ὀργῇ, οὐ τύχῃ οὐδεμιᾷ, ὃ μὴ οἷόν τ' ἔσται λῦσαι τῷ Διονύσῳ, that is used to request the encosmic ruler, Dionysos, for cleansing and a release from bonds. It translates to, "Nothing can be so firmly bound by illness, wrath, or fortune, that cannot be released by Dionysos" (Krasskova, 2017). It is highly effective in prayers and rituals.

- Drew Campbell, who published a book in 2000 about the adoption of theistic practice centered around Hellenic Gods in the United States, created several chants for Gods, including Zeus, Artemis, Athene, and Hera, drawing from inspiration and ancient texts.[5] I sing the one to Artemis when I pray to her, although I use a different melody.

Keep in mind that the Gods I worship are primarily Hellenic, so I have been drawn to phrases in Greek or translated from Greek into English. You can identify chants and prayers for your own practice that draw from the sources that make the

---

[5]You can find these on the Internet Archive. Here is the website as it looked in 2012.
https://web.archive.org/web/20120506135235/https://www.ecauldron.net/dc-mousike.php

most sense to you. The author of *Ásatrú for Beginners* recommends several phrases from Norse source texts to use in ritual; he suggests them as prayers, but they are short enough to use for chanting, too (Nordvig, 2020: 63). A few sets of prayer beads I purchased came with prayers, and I use those prayers (with modifications) for Eir, Belesama, Apollon, Hermes, and several other Gods. After chanting for several minutes, I come into stillness while maintaining mental focus on the God. When focus is very hard, I visualize the actual words of the chant, which makes a big difference for me.

Sometimes, I don't start with prayer beads. I start by reading a poem — a hymn translation from the ancient world or a more recent composition — for the God or thinking about aspects of the God in epithets and culture before I drop into stillness. Epithets, or devotional titles, are common in many cultures. For example, Apollon can be called the Far-Shooter or He Who Wards From Afar. They often come from place-names, mythic associations, or something that the God is considered to be especially good at, and they can be chanted in either the original language or something else. I find that this is grounding — like the image, it improves my focus. Depending on when I do this during the day, I may light incense or give the God a libation.

You may want to take some notes on chants you want to investigate based on the God(s) you are considering praying to. Hold onto this for the chapter on doing research or go ahead and get started — it's up to you.

Contemplating a Text

Contemplating a text is a classic in many religious and spiritual traditions. It can be done in a traditional meditation; with a pen and paper at a desk; or at a computer — airplane your phone, turn off all notifications, and ensure that you are difficult to contact while you're working through your thoughts. Spending a few minutes with a task before you go on a walk or bringing a reading with you to the gym are also great options. While I sometimes contemplate passages from Platonic texts immediately after my morning prayers, my days are too hectic to do that all of the time, so I usually think about passages from what I'm reading while doing dishes or commuting. You know if you are a restless thinker who needs to be doing something tactile while your mind is working.

To start, say a small, heartfelt prayer to the God(s) in the myth or text. Read the passage you want to work with and jot down what comes to mind. Highlight any passages you want to spend extra attention on, and pause whenever inspiration strikes. You can come back to the same text many times. You can use specific passages from your notes as seeds for a seated meditation. Sometimes, if you alternate between taking notes on myths and contemplating a divine image, elements of the myth will arise spontaneously in the mind while you are doing the seated meditation on the God.

Breathwork and Adapted Meditation Techniques

For those who have exposure to and practice with other forms of meditation, doing pranayama/breathwork or using meditation techniques like body scans, noting, lovingkindness, and so on can sometimes be adapted to a contemplative spiritual practice like this.

Headspace, Calm, and other meditation apps have guided tutorials on these techniques, and YouTube is another option. Pranayama techniques are from South Asian religious traditions, and people most frequently pick them up from attending a yoga class in person or online. Look up local opportunities in your area if possible.

There are also techniques called "grounding and centering" that I learned growing up. A person envisions that they are rooted into the ground like a tree, drawing up nourishment from the Earth, and drawing down energy from the sun or sun and stars as the central point of this structure. It can be beneficial to do techniques like that if one is feeling scattered and distracted. Grounding and centering techniques are used in a variety of modern spiritual and religious traditions because they work well. You can find guided exercises made by people from a variety of backgrounds on YouTube. Local pagan and polytheist groups may also teach these techniques during open-to-the-public rituals, if they have any.

Sometimes, I do breath of fire (a pranayama technique, kapalbhati) before contemplating a God. I do meditative visualizations in which sunlight, starlight, or moonlight are filling the body, depending on the context — honoring the solstice or full moon, for example.

2.4   Ritual Practices

Ritual practices are everywhere in contemporary culture — glossy checkout magazines, online-only publications offering the gamut of self-care options, pop culture spirituality blogs, mainstream occult practices, corporate cultish bonding exercises, and so on. One app I have used in the past for personal development sometimes called my morning, workday, and evening routines "rituals" — and there wasn't even a preexisting option for adding prayer to a routine.

In *The Soul's Inner Statues*, we will use "ritual" for any activities we do to connect with Gods, divinities, and those who have come before us. A ritual in this context is a set of routine practices we use in this context.

It is possible to pray without something being a ritual. Sometimes, when I am outside after work in the winter, I see the rising full moon, and I often murmur a quick prayer or press my fingertips to my lips and forehead to acknowledge the lunar Gods. There is no ritual involved in that spontaneous reverence, and honestly, it's fine to keep some practices simple.

2.5   Hearth, Home, and Ancestors

Who you pray to out of affinity — this God, that Goddess, someone else — are often like friendships that change and fade over time. A few are continuous, and many are transient. Household worship is very different because you live somewhere. Even if you are in a liminal space — without a home, living in a dorm, or traveling — there are Gods who preside over liminal spaces who can be deeply enriching to pray to.

The core of household worship is making offerings to household Gods, often a hearth Goddess and one or more divinities who preside over things like property, storerooms, and abundance.[6] Examples of household divinities are the Penates (Roman), house wights (various places), Agathos Daimon (Greek, meaning "good spirit/intermediary"), Tykhe or Fortuna (Greek and Roman), the Kitchen God (Chinese folk religion), or a household-focused aspect of a God. Every God technically is a unique perspective on the entirety of everything, so you *could* worship any of them as your household God. However, the specific preexisting associations people have made between a God and a set of activities are powerful expressions of how that God operates in the world. They are also easiest to "tap into" for people who have never worshipped Gods before. Some Gods with well-established household aspects, like Apollon, Zeus, and Hermes, have specific household functions — Zeus of the Storeroom, for example, is literally the God who keeps your cozy duvet inserts and tea safe; Apollon of the Streets protects public spaces and harmonizes the home with the exterior world through the threshold boundary. Hermes, as a liminal God, is highly relevant to boundaries. The Norse Goddess Frigg and the Goddesses associated with her (the Handmaidens) have associations with many domestic tasks.

Household worship can involve considerations of one's

---

[6]Indeed, we could characterize the reverence of many Gods *as* connected to and anchored in our homes. A stylized hearthfire symbol is the perfect symbol to characterize what *The Soul's Inner Statues* aims to achieve, as it symbolizes the hearth and the divine flame within us.

ancestors of affinity, culture, or personal heritage. Depending on your ancestry and your relationship with said ancestors, this will likely cause mixing and matching. For most people, including me, it is not an instantaneous thing — it builds slowly over time, woven by synchronicity and effort and duty.

As an example, let me tell you about my own fact-finding mission. After deciding to bring my practice more in alignment with my values, for some months, I experimented with praying to Frigg (Nordic), Nantosuelta and Brigando (both Gaulish), and Hestia (Greek) as hearth Goddesses. I primarily worship the Hellenic Gods (but I am not Greek), and I started exploring what it would be like to pray to household deities related to my roots. While the Neopagan community I had grown up in had done a lot for Brigid (who is related to Brigando), that prayer practice wasn't fruitful — it felt forced. I reevaluated what I was doing through a combination of thinking, ranting in journals, and divination. Ultimately, after a contemplative experience in which I felt Hestia's presence very powerfully, and after months of not having that in the way I was trying to blend everything, I realized that Hestia, and her Roman counterpart Vesta, whom I identify with Hestia strongly (not everyone does), was the bedrock of my hearth. Frigg and Nantosuelta are also important to me — Frigg is the Goddess I think of when I think of my matrilineal ancestors' strength, and Nantosuelta reminds me of the fecundity of the apple country close to my heart in Upstate New York, where my maternal family is from and where I spent my childhood. They are important household Goddesses for me, too. As a Platonizing polytheist, revering Hestia makes sense with where

I am coming from. This is much more harmonious.

Now, what do I mean by *fact-finding mission*? It means deliberately putting yourself into a new situation and actually trying something, trusting that the Gods will lead you where you need to be. Whenever I make ritual changes, I usually give it a few weeks for me to settle into the new routine. New routines are always a bit awkward in the beginning! Then, I pay attention to signs in my body, emotions, mental impressions and experiences, and serendipitous things that happen during ritual and ask myself if these are signs that my spiritual practice is in a *good state* or if it's not clicking. A persistent feeling of frustration is generally a sign that it isn't working out well. Some will do divination or seek specialist help when working through this. As shown in the example, I usually do journaling and brainstorming, and I have a very deep spiritual reading practice that often illuminates what could work better right when I need it.

It is *perfectly fine* to do fact-finding or to not be sure about where one will land when one is just starting out — or even to revisit long-held practices that one never worked through systematically before.

For reflection:

- Do you already know of any hearth deities? What about home divinities?

- Who interests you the most? Look them up. Wikipedia has a list of hearth deities around the world that can be helpful — just check the Talk page if you want to see what went into contributors' creation of the page (Wikipedia contributors, 2022).

2.5.1   Home During College

Household worship, from a practical standpoint, can be very simple. I have maintained a sacred space in my living area since I was twelve or so. In eighth grade, I made a bench in shop class that became my small floor-level shrine until I went to college, when I lived in the dorms. Incense and candles were forbidden for fire safety reasons, but I often had a small space on my bookshelf that was marked as "sacred" — even if I often neglected it. As most young adult students do, I moved a lot: dorm room to dorm room, apartment to apartment, between my family's home and transient student spaces, and my spiritual life was like an untamed, rowdy horse. You can *still* have hearth deities during this period of your life and keep a shrine, even if it is very simple. Libations and electric candles go a long way. You may, however, prefer to focus on deities related to education, especially if you are living in a dorm setting. There wasn't much advice on how to be disciplined about a spiritual practice in new adulthood when I was young; hopefully this book helps future generations.

2.5.2   Worship Without Being Creepy About Heritage

In Rumi's "The Guest House," the poet frames our lives as transitory places:

> This being human is a guest house.
> Every morning a new arrival.
>
> A joy, a depression, a meanness,
> some momentary awareness comes
> as an unexpected visitor. (Rumi, n.d.)

Even before I encountered that poem, I had been contemplating the idea of our lives as temporary places. As someone who reads Plato and who holds to Platonic teachings about reincarnation, I know that our families, lineages, and personal contexts change from lifetime to lifetime. There is no steadiness in them. Parodoxically, in Plato and the Platonists, there is a strong emphasis on meeting the context of your current life where it is and paying your respect to Gods and ancestors. This dates back to Epictetus the Stoic and to Plato. However, this is ideally like being a guest in someone's house: the family may last a long time, and so may your region's people and/or culture, but *you* will not be there forever. You need to leave the family better than you found it, and you need to be mindful that the family is not *you* — you are an incarnating soul.

When I started to embark on incorporating ancestral practices, it was important to me to do it without being creepy — it's contextual to this lifetime, so how does that translate into practice? The ultimate goal for anyone incorporating such practices is to ensure that one is not neglecting important divinities and Gods. Reaching out to ancestral deities is an act of repair for those of us whose ancestors ruptured ties to Gods by converting to an evangelizing, one-true-way religion. In the popular TV series *The Good Place*, interpersonal obligations were built up through the phrase "what do we owe each other?" — also the title of a philosophical book that presumably is working through what our web of connections and obligations mean. The way it played out on the TV show involved characters learning etiquette and mutual respect. If we want to set boundaries between ourselves and absolutism and intolerance, changing one's worldview **from** one of either rootlessness or clinging attachment **to** a worldview of *repair* and *compassionate duty* can work wonders. Obviously, there are many times when the answer to "should I be worshipping you, Gods who may have been worshipped by my great-great-great-great-great grandparents?" is no, and that's fine. There are plenty of people who have satisfying spiritual lives joining a tradition that has nothing to do with where they are from.

Because we are worshipping Gods and divinities who are individuals and not archetypes, an analogy can be drawn to reaching out to family after an estrangement you inherited from your parents — it may be awkward, it may fail, but it's worth it to phone and see what happens. For example, if one's ancestors lived in areas where they likely had a Lararium (a household shrine for the Lares) eighteen hundred years ago, trying that out again may be a useful first step. If your family now lives in an area where people had Lararia eighteen hundred years ago, but you ultimately trace your roots elsewhere, you should also feel empowered to explore having one — you live there *now*, regardless of your ancestors' origins, so it's part of your cultural history, too. Ancestry is an amalgam of personal heritage and cultural heritage. Real human beings are messy, and we do not fit into boxes.

There are other ways our current incarnation can impact us. In the *Phaedrus* commentary taken down by Hermias during one of the Platonist Syrianus' lectures fifteen hundred years ago, the text comments that someone will often reincarnate into a family to resolve injustices from generations ago (Hermias, 2018). When we incarnate, we pick what is best for our soul given our options. What is best for us as souls could include repairing such ruptures and the harm caused by previous generations. *We are in a guest house:* Doing this is for the good of everyone, no strings attached, so the fact that we may not incarnate into the group benefitting from our hard work should not deter us from doing the correct thing now.

In other words, reaching for ancestral traditions is healthy when it comes out of a desire to do what is just and to repair what was broken or cast aside. We repair our relationship with the Gods and we commit to transmitting it to those who come after us. We should ask ourselves *how, why, and for whom* as prompts to deepen our practice without succumbing to hate, division, and false senses of superiority. Questions like these can also heal a disorienting sense of unplacing when they are approached from a place of compassion, fierce honesty, and care. While the answers may create some very personalized practices, the process will lead to a personalized ritual practice that is *solidly grounded in piety* according to what is most just in each person or family's specific case.

Admittedly, in some cases, Gods were transmitted to us from another culture so many generations ago that they feel like ours, and we need to be mindful about recognizing that the living descendants of the ancient cultures they come from have their own histories and relationships to the same Gods — it's part of being culturally and globally aware. In America, most of us, regardless of our background, trace our cultural history to what was going on in Britain four hundred to two hundred years ago when they were an imperial power taking everything from everybody. Those of us (non-Greek) Americans who worship Greek/Hellenic Gods do so because British people really liked them during the Renaissance and Early Modern period, and fluency in Greek literature and its motifs proved someone was cultured even after the texts started to be translated into English. Greece is 1800 miles away from England. It is a very different culture. The same goes for Britain's Egypt craze and its impact on the accessibility of information about Egyptian Gods. Chaldeans, Assyrians, Hellenes, and other identifiers we read about in history books are the names of cultural and/or ethnic groups that still exist today.

2.5.3   Today Is Not Yesterday

Iamblichus wrote in V.25 of *On the Mysteries* that the traditions are not "just a matter of human customs" driven by convention. Rather than originating from us, the "God is the initiator of these things, he who is called 'the god who presides over sacrifices,' and there is also a great multitude of gods and angels in attendance upon him." Every holy place, people, or sacrifice has a divine leader such that "when we perform our sacrifices to the gods with the backing of gods as supervisors and executives of the sacrificial procedure, we should on the one hand pay due reverence to the regulation of the sanctity of divine sacrifice, but on the other we may have due confidence in ourselves" because we are approaching the Gods as the Gods intended us to. Iamblichus cautioned against changing names and ritual elements.

Simplicius, when discussing the best way to venerate the Gods according to the Stoic Epictetus, echoes what Iamblichus said:

> We must perform everything that pertains to di-
> vine honour with purity, and not in a slovenly way
> [...]. Nor should we do any of these things with-
> out care, [Epictetus] says, so that we omit one of
> the necessary parts, or confuse things, or change
> them, through negligence. If you delete the let-
> ters of a word, or rearrange them, the form of the
> word does not occur; similarly in the case of di-
> vine words and deeds, if anything is left out, or
> rearranged, or confused, divine illumination does
> not occur — instead, the negligence of the one per-
> forming the ritual waters down the power of the
> events (Simplicius, 2014: 67).

When you read the words above, keep in mind that the situation in Late Antiquity when Iamblichus (who died in 325
CE) and Simplicius (alive in the 500s CE) were active was not
the same as ours. Case in point: You are reading this book to
figure out how to pray, but if we had had no disruption, you
would have learned this from the adults around you when you
were a toddler. That is one reason why this book is free (if
you're reading it online) or priced at the cost of materials and
distribution (if you're reading the print).

Whereas we only have the names and ephemeral archaeological evidence for some Gods, our predecessors usually had
access to a lot of contextual information. A person worshipping back then had deep connections to the rites conducted
in a region, rituals that often predated historical records. As

Christianity spread throughout the Mediterranean and into Europe, the Middle East, and Africa, the destruction of temples, cultural heritage materials, divine images, and our connection with the Gods our ancestors worshipped has led to a colossal amount of knowledge destruction. This violent iconoclasm and loss is ongoing in places that are targeted by Christian missionaries for conversion, often upheld by toxic Western narratives about "primitive" people and practices.

To worship Gods, many of us are taking a look at fragments of what was once practiced — small traces of Gods' worship in historical times — and using our best judgment to apply what we know about that to the present day. We are identifying how we can move forward. In addition, many of us encounter Gods in places very alien to the original context in which they were worshipped — how do we know Inanna after reading *Gilgamesh* or Artemis after perusing Callimachus when we have no other connection to them? We are starting fresh from our own context.

Sometimes, a person can get lost in the weeds of historical record and miss the object: connecting with a God. They view the words above as being directed at *us* and not at the contemporaries of the ancient philosophers. Simplicius continues:

> What is most important is the concentrated eagerness of the agent, along with [their] knowledge, as it is with the fulfilment and perfection of other things. But how can someone who is patently careless and negligent about things concerning [the] God be in earnest about anything that is necessary? Nor is it right for us to approach 'impiously',

he says, — that is, without reverence. For the more
honourable and worthy of reverence we consider
the divine rituals to be, the more we participate in
them as such; and if we subordinate ourselves, in
so far as we are able, to the reverence of [the] God,
then we too are magnified (Simplicius, 2014: 67).

It is very clear that Simplicius' main concern is people slacken-
ing away from the rites at the time in an environment where
frequently only a few people retained the knowledge of what
had, before Christianity, been widespread practices for Gods.
It was also eventually illegal to engage in the worship of Gods
in the Roman Empire, although many tenacious people risked
their lives to preserve piety. This was also Iamblichus' concern, albeit the situation had not reached a crisis point in his
lifetime — his theological writing is a highly respected work
for those interested in the theology of many Gods.

Ultimately, we are not the ancients, and our goal is to
establish a connection to the Gods we want to worship *here*, in
our own cultural contexts. We can draw what we can from the
past, we can pray for insight from the Gods to find the right
rituals and words for our liturgies and daily practices, and we
can look to living cultures to get an idea of what adaptations
to the modern world religions have.

The techniques I am providing for prayer in *The Soul's Inner
Statues* are grounded in today, in the *now* of the Gods. They
are designed to be as general as possible (although I know
that my Platonizing perspective has an impact on how I frame
this advice), and to help you think about your own customized
practice in part. We cannot go back. In the 21st century, it is

important to look forward and adapt to our environments.

We are also given this by Simplicius to encourage us to think about our own lived context:

> 'It is fitting' for each of us to do these things according to the customs of one's country. For [the] God is always simultaneously present everywhere, with all of his divine powers. But we are limited to one form among those many forms produced by [the] God, the human form, and within the human form are limited to one form of life for now and one choice of life, and are divided up into a little portion of the universe and of the earth itself. So different people partake in a different instances of divine goodness, and they do so in a different way at different times and places. You can at least see that when it is day with us, it is night for others, and when it is winter in one place, it is summer in another, and that these sorts of flora and fauna prevail here, and elsewhere other sorts: the earth and the things on it partake of divine goodness in a divided way. So, just as the places and lives of people differ, each person propitiates the divine through the rites which God revealed and which they themselves became aware of through experience, rites which differ in their occasions and methods, and in the variation of the objects sacrificed and offered. And when the affairs of [the] God are celebrated according to [the] God, a particular activity of divine illumination becomes

evident on certain circumscribed days which is not at all evident on other days: the sick are cured, and sometimes some beneficial events are foretold. A difference of time, or the consonance of place and method with what is uttered, wrought and offered — all of these have a great effect on divine assimilation (Simplicius, 2014: 66–67).

To adapt the worship of the Gods to today, we need to live the spirit of what Simplicius said about the need to revere and honor the divine rituals — we want to build something new that we can share forward as the new bedrock of the future.

- Start by **researching** Gods — we will cover some tips on successful adult learning in a few chapters, but for now, pay attention to the traditional associations and symbols. As you work through the chapters of this book, if you jot down notes about any deities you want to worship, use that space to collect small pieces of information about their traditional festivals, the types of symbols they are shown with, any divine nicknames (epithets) they have, and so on. Check for information about how these Gods were culturally transmitted into your region. Was it in antiquity? The Renaissance? After World War II? Are they from your area? A combination?

- Once you have researched, start **reflecting**. Brainstorm how those descriptors relate to your own lived experience. Think about new directions based on your region or the history of how the Gods became known to your area. Also consider specific customs you have in your culture and ways the God(s) could be brought into conversation with those.

- Pray to the Gods for assistance in **designing** your home practice. Use this information to select the ritual elements and traditions you want to start with, what you will offer, and when you will do offerings.

- Start **listening**. Establishing something from scratch is iterative. It is a conversation between you and the Gods. If you feel stuck, go back to the reflection and design stages. Writing this book helped me work through a lot in my own practice, and I have gone through five or six iterations of my daily household ritual in the past year! It's okay to be a work in progress as long as your goal is authentic, open-hearted reverence of the Gods.

If you follow these bullet points, you will be well on your way to mitigating the problems with getting lost in the past. Focus on rootedness, and remember that trees' roots are not deep the moment they sprout. Many things of deep value in this world take time and careful attention.

Please note that you are not expected to do all of the above immediately. Bookmark this section to glance at when you do the exercises at the end of the next few chapters.

What About the Awful Things?

While the initiator of rites is a God, human beings can never perfectly receive what is intended by the Gods. When we look at archaeological evidence, the written record, and other sources, we may notice that the ancient world was sometimes a brutal place, and this occasionally shows up in religious practice or the analogies that philosophers use when talking about first principles. Slavery, treating women like chattel, overly punitive legal codes, and other social evils were rampant.

Specific places' social inequality structures are not things that the Gods are responsible for, and indeed, the closer we look, the more we discover that the past's relationship with its own evils is complex. In the Platonic tradition, evils are a phantasmic, not-really-real, parasitic occurrence caused by the extreme spatio-temporal partiality of the natural and material world. As our behaviors and social norms are parts of the natural world, the ways we venerate Gods are no exception.

The generations that created these traditions may have had very poignant insights about the divine. As our predecessors were human beings, just as we are human, it was just as easy for them to ignore heinous injustices they were habituated to accept from youth as it is for *us* to ignore the injustices of our own time. (How many of us are wearing clothes or using devices that may have been produced by human trafficking or child labor?) However, pushing back against these evils is not a new thing. The bhakti movement in South Asia had factions, still existing today, that worship Gods like Shiva, believe in the spiritual equality of men and women to the point of having no menstrual taboos, and despite casteism; this dates back at least a millennium. Women in Mediterranean Late Antiquity suffered from harsh sexism. However, in Platonic and other philosophical schools, girls were educated and could even grow up to teach, like Sosipatra and Hypatia, because Plato

taught that women have the same virtues as men, and philosophers seemed to take the idea of educating their daughters
seriously. There have always been resistances and fresh, pious directions for people to take because the Gods are good.
They open up these ways for us even if our broader societies
don't always embrace them.

Often, people look at the past and are struck still — angry,
often shocked — by it all. It's our job to learn from this messi-
ness to tell the narratives we want to tell and to crown our
ancestors — literal, spiritual, or elsewise — through the power
of our informed, pious actions in the present.

When we light incense or give a libation at a household
shrine, we are all equal to one another. The Gods do not dis-
criminate based on your race, ethnicity, social class, disability
status, sex, sexual orientation, gender, caste, and so on. When
we pray, we are praying as souls reaching out to a God. All
of us belong. Plotinus encouraged each of us to never stop
working on our statue — to always be willing to be better. That
is what actually matters.

As we build the rhythms of our fresh traditions, coaxing
them out of the Earth like a holy plant that has just germinated,
we can ground this growing relationship in trust. The way
to interpret what Iamblichus said about the Gods starting
these rites — in terms of us *today* — is to *genuinely* focus on
the God as the starting point. Have trust in the practice and
in the process. Read about the Gods, learn and apply the
information about virtue and conduct in later chapters, and
keep the Gods at the center of any corrections and changes
you make to rituals. We can always ensure that the core keeps

its integrity even if peripheral elements change — such as who in the family is considered the *paterfamilias* in a gay or lesbian marriage, whether or not it is appropriate for us to adapt a specific ancient festival to a private ceremony in our home today, and so on.

Ultimately, your practice is your practice. What you do at your shrine, as long as you are being a respectful, pious, and decent person, is just as good as anyone else's effort. Sometimes, people who love their Gods, but who face harm from other devotees, think that they need to choose between remaining in a specific community and receiving abuse and leaving and losing the Gods. No matter how hard it is, you can always leave and bring the Gods you love with you. Your personal or family shrine is *yours*. Take responsibility for it.

2.6 Practice

In the introduction, I recommended clearing off a shelf or small space to use for a household shrine. It is time to make use of this space.

You need:

- Something for pouring liquid.

- Something to pour liquid into.

- The name of the deity you're worshipping — either a post-it note or something fancier. (I often use popsicle sticks, and I will use colorful markers to make them look nice.)

That's it.

Often, especially when we're looking at ritual space stock photography or the spaces of people who have committed disposable income to pricier items, we see beautiful statuary and intricate spaces. This helps, but it's not necessary — and, given the climate crisis, it makes sense to be measured about purchases instead of contributing to overconsumption. Once you have a good idea that you want to worship a God and have maintained the habit for long enough, go ahead and think about images.

The bare minimum you need for worshipping a God is their name. In antiquity, when people were pouring libations and making sacrifices on altars, the altar was marked with the name of the God or Gods. It is like having someone's address in the *to:* field when you send an email.

For a hearth deity, I also recommend a small candle or flame representation. You can use a traditional lighter or a rechargeable electric lighter. Some people even use electric candles! There are phone apps that mimic fires and candles, too.

For a libation, any drink is fine — even water. I sometimes buy loose dried tulsi and make a concentrate that I store in the refrigerator. Whenever I want to pray, I pour some into the libation jar I use and add water. I also offer a flavored water concentrate that I like, especially to my ancestral Gods — it feels very intimate to share beverages I actually drink. Some people offer wine or other alcohols. I find that I don't go through the bottles quickly enough to use up all of the alcohol before it goes off, and since I rarely drink, it feels odd to give a God something that isn't part of my diet unless the deity has a symbolic relationship with alcohol.

Other types of offerings include incenses, flowers, and food. If you use incense, be careful of resins — do not burn them indoors on charcoal disks, as there is a carbon monoxide risk. Always be in a well-ventilated area. Burning resins outdoors with a fire-safe setup is fine. Stick and cone incense are great for daily indoor use, and some companies sell low-smoke incense. If you use essential oils in an oil diffuser in your offering space, please check that your oil is pet-safe if you have animals — vets have been more public in recent years about what to choose and avoid. Never use citrus oils around your cat. Be careful about flame-based oil diffusers, as they can be a fire risk.

Disposing of offerings can be done in a clean sink (for libations) or in your household trash. If you offer food or flowers, the most respectful way to put them in your waste receptacle is to wrap them in paper (like a used grocery bag from the time you forgot your reusable bags, padding paper left over from a package, or similar) and add them to the trash just before you put it out curbside. If you can compost, that is preferred, but don't worry if you can't — I, too, live in an apartment without that option. If you offer non-fresh goods like dried flowers or wreaths, rotating them out after six months to a year is auspicious — especially if you do it at about the time of the winter or summer solstice.

Sometimes, people eat the food offerings shortly after they are offered — the food is now blessed by the God(s), and eating it is the completion of the reciprocal relationship. Traditionally, some practices (i.e., for Gods worshipped in Egypt) have done this by default. In other areas, it has been common according to custom for the Gods' portion to be separated from what everyone will eat. Do what seems right to you, except for underworld Gods — see the chapter on Purification for more details.

Specific scents, herbs, plants, foods, and other material objects may be sacred to a God. If you want to be sure that your prayer space has the correct ambiance, lean into those correspondences. It is very easy to Google *[name of deity] what to offer* and end up with creative ideas from people of all ages, experience levels, and backgrounds. I have offered Apollon bay leaves, and I usually offer frankincense incense to him when I do something more elaborate. You may also develop intuition over time that tells you a specific offering is a good one. I use an incense blend called River Path for some Gods because the incense's name evokes the connection I aim to establish.

If you are setting up a permanent space, be respectful. Never use your shrine as a landing space for random objects and clutter. Encourage family members and/or roommates to avoid putting anything there that isn't an offering.

Now, do you need to worry about getting the "wrong God" or "summoning" something else? People coming from modern occultism may have encountered this idea, and it is not relevant here. We are setting aside a sacred space using the names and symbols of the God, the Gods are wholly good, and daily shrine prayers are a foundational practice that people do around the world. This is normative and safe.

2.6.1 Household Prayer

Hopefully, you now have a shelf or another location where you can create a pop-up or long-term prayer space. If you have purchased or gathered any items, now is the time to place them there. Clean and arrange them in an ergonomically useful way.

Before praying, I recommend washing your hands. If you are praying after your daily shower, congratulations on habit-stacking.

If you have a candle or other flame representation, light it or turn it on. Keep your elbows at your sides and hold out your forearms with your hands palm-up. Standing up is the common practice, although one can sit if necessary.

Say something like:

> I honor and acknowledge the household Gods, [insert any specific names]. I give you this offering of [whatever you're offering].

Make the offering. If you are doing a libation, this means pouring whatever you have chosen to offer into the bowl. Sometimes, after offering most of something, a person will take a sip of the remainder.

Take a pause and a few deep breaths.

If you are honoring specific Gods and divinities and know anything about them, this is the time to call to mind those aspects. For Nantosuelta, for example, one might think of her connection to beehives, fire, fertility, apples, and Earth — far from just being a Goddess of the home, she has many areas of affinity that are not related to the home in the slightest.

Sometimes, people will recite poems they've found about the deities and divinities they're worshipping, play music, or speak from the heart about what they have going on in their lives. You could do that now if you like.

When done, say:

> Thank you, [insert any specific names or just say "household God(s)"]. May you bless me, my family, my friends, and my communities with whatever is most good, fitting, and appropriate.

Dispose of the offering in a few hours. I like to clean out my offering bowls after I've done dishes in the evening.

2.6.2   Meditation

This meditation is based on an exercise from one of Plotinus' *Enneads* and on a meditation that I've done since I was a teenager.

The passage from Plotinus' *Enneads* is at 5.8.9, and here's how it is translated by Gerson (note that the pronoun "he" is used for the God, but this could be any deity):

> So, let us grasp by discursive thinking this cosmos all together as one, each of its parts remaining what it is and not jumbled together, if possible, so that if any one of these should occur to us — for example, the sphere outside the periphery of the cosmos — an image of the sun follows immediately and together with it all the other stars, and earth and sea and all the living beings are seen, as if all

these were in reality to be seen in a transparent sphere. Let there be formed in your soul, then, the image of a luminous sphere having all things in it, whether moving or stable, or some moving and some stable.

Keeping this image, take another for yourself by abstracting the mass from it. Abstract, too, places and the semblance of the matter you have in yourself. Don't try to take another sphere smaller than it in mass, but call on the god who made that of which you have a semblance, and pray for him to come. And he might come bearing his cosmos with all of the gods in it, being one and all of them, and each is all coming together as one, each with different powers, though all are one by that multiple single power. Rather, it is that one god who is all. For he lacks nothing, if all those gods should become what they are. They are all together and each is separate, again, in indivisible rest, having no sensible shape — for if they had, one would be in one place, and one in another, and each would not have all in himself. Nor do they have different parts in different places, nor all in the identical place, nor is each whole like a power fragmented, being quantifiable, like measured parts. It is rather all power, extending without limit, being unlimited in power. And in this way, the god is great, as the parts of it are all unlimited. For where could one say that he is not already present? (Plotinus,

2018: 5.8.9)

For this prayer, place a chair or cushion near your shrine to use as a meditation seat. Make a short prayer:

> I pray to the Gods and give you this offering before
> my meditation. May you be well disposed.

or

> I pray to [deity] and ask for your guidance during
> this meditation.

If you have an offering, make it now, and then be seated.

For this meditation, start off by doing a body scan, eyes closed or open. Start the scan at the top of your head, working through parts of the body to see what is comfortable or uncomfortable. Notice the pressure of gravity and the places where you are touching the floor or chair.

Once you have finished the body scan, turn your attention to the boundary between your skin and the air. Envision your awareness expanding from your body and into the room around you. Feel the furniture and become aware of the life within your home. From there, expand your awareness steadily to every room in your home or apartment. If you are in an apartment, expand your awareness to the entire building.

From your building, steadily come to encompass the neighborhood, then the city, and finally your region. Allow your awareness to expand in awareness until you are holding the world in your mind. Examine the differences in climate and ground cover, sunlight levels and depth of night. Rest here for a moment.

When you are ready, expand it outward from the Earth to the Earth-Moon system. Grow through the void to reach the planets of the inner solar system and the Sun, then the asteroid belt and the outer planets, and finally the mass of smaller bodies that make up the frozen fringes of the solar system. Expand your awareness to the nearest star systems, then to the galaxy. Know that we are in a network of galaxies, and expand into that. Eventually, your awareness will encompass all of the honeycombed web of the universe. It is filled with voids and oases of light.

All of this has evolved in time, and it came from a point of indescribably high density. The visible universe was once about the size of a grapefruit. You are containing at least all of this within your awareness.

Now, think of all that you are holding within your mind, and call to mind what it would be without mass. Call to mind all that is, and then imagine it spaceless. Contract all that you have become aware of without giving it mass, shape, or extent in time. Beyond the spatial extent, beyond time, and beyond bodies, there is an inflection point of divinity. As Plotinus wrote so long ago, ask for the God to come.

Whatever comes to your awareness, rest with it until you judge the meditation to be finished. Thank the Gods and put back your chair or cushion.

This exercise is a bit different from what is happening in Plotinus' *Ennead* 5.8.9, as it fuses the abstraction of his words and their beauty with an expansion into everything visible around us. However, it can still be a powerful visualization practice. If visualization isn't right for you, I encourage you to replace this with another meditation technique.

2.7   Time Blocking Exercise

In the above practices, you have done a ritual prayer and embarked on the opening of the way to your soul's inner statues — a beautiful thing to be celebrated. It may feel new, different, and give you a sense of calm (at least, once the awkward feeling of newness fades) — but chances are, you figured out a time to do these exercises that fits into your daily routine.

I recommend doing prayers right after you shower (or whichever freshening up activity you do every day). The chapter on purification will discuss that in more depth and will give you an opportunity to create backup scenarios for when life gets hectic.

Now, though, I want you to think about your morning, afternoon, or evening routine — whichever time you think it is best to pray. And I want you to time block it.

Time blocking could involve post-it notes, notecards, or a piece of paper. You could also use a digital post-it app like Mural, a workflow diagram generator, or anything else you are comfortable with.

Think of what your routine is like for the time of day you have chosen. Write down each step, including the amount of time it takes you. This is a private activity. Please do not treat yourself as your aspirational self. If you make your coffee/tea and stand there by your French press entranced by your Twitter feed for twenty minutes, or if you're on your phone playing Candy Crush on the toilet for ten, note that down.

Once you have a realistic image of your routine, you can think about what you want to adjust. The rituals we are discussing in *The Soul's Inner Statues* can be as swift as two to five minutes. Can you wake up five minutes earlier, or is there time you can adjust? Are there other aspects of your routine that you're unhappy with?

Work through your routine until you find something that is both satisfying and actionable. Transfer the information to a physical sheet of paper (one or two is ideal) and put it where you will see it at that time of day.

Try not to change too much — for habit-building, the most lasting change is incremental. Once you have made good progress on this for a few weeks, go back to your notes about your routine and pick one other thing to shift. For example, if you want to read more, ensure that there's a book by your coffee/tea setup instead of your phone. If you need a few more minutes to pray or meditate, add that in.

As someone who prays in the morning, avoiding social media, email, and my to-do list is what works for me so I can have that extra prayer time. Because I pray for longer than five minutes, I also wake up earlier — at 6:15 AM instead of 6:45 AM. I like having time to give prayers to a variety of Gods, including Gods of the sacred day in the calendar system I learned in my early 20s, and to sit in contemplation for at least a few minutes. However, I do have that quick ritual routine in my back pocket if I oversleep. Often, I do prayer beads or a quick prayer and meditation after I brush my teeth and before

I go to bed, which lasts only a few minutes unless an idea for a poem comes to me. The timing of your prayer is up to you.

Chapter 3

Gods

We devoted much of the last chapter to discussing some foundational aspects of a spiritual practice for many Gods, and we ended with practices that anyone can integrate into their life: a few moments of worship at home, both prayer and contemplation. In this chapter, we will build on those practices and pick one or two more Gods to worship — for now, no more than that.[1]

It is not necessary to worship every single God every day (that would be impossible), just as one cannot be friends with every human being in the world or every sentient being in the cosmos. Beyond worshipping the household Gods and divinities, and perhaps doing ancestor worship on auspicious

---

[1]Sometimes, a person may decide to pray to a collective of Gods: the Muses, for example, or the Fates, Matronae, Attendants of Frigg, Gods of Civic Discourse, Storm Gods, and so on. In my personal practice, I usually pray to the Muses as a collective. Others may devote prayers to all of the Gods in general — often using names and terminology relevant to a specific cultural grouping of Gods, such as the twelve Olympians in Plato's *Phaedrus* or a set of major Roman, Nordic, Celtic, Gaulish, Sumerian, or other deities.

days for such activities, most people only have the bandwidth for a handful of Gods and divinities before their attention is too scattered to have a deep and meaningful practice. *The Soul's Inner Statues* is focused on breaking down the steps to work towards a manageable, meaningful practice, so this chapter approaches embarking on that in chunks through steady, sustained change.

Keeping the number of Gods limited at first helps you settle into a concise prayer routine, and it allows for mindful expansion of your practice if you judge that expanding it is important to you. Billions of people around the world pray for only a few minutes a day. The most important thing, and the hardest, is showing up.

As you read this chapter, take some notes on what comes up for you. The exercise at the end will ask you to look up one or two Gods and to pray to them.

3.1   How Do You Pick a God?

The factors involved in choosing Gods to worship are many. In this section, we will discuss a few major ones.

Culture and region. For many people, this is what is done: You worship the God whose temple is down the street (or whose ruins are in your area) or Gods who are widely present in your cultural substrate, whether or not your culture writ large worships them. In the United States, specific regions, cities, and states may use the images of specific Classical Gods or Goddesses, and revering them is possible. Outside of the United States, there may be temples and cultural sites (ruins or still in use) that could inspire you. You may even be able to join local groups.

Following what a group does. People raised in a specific religious group, or who join a group as an adult that honors specific deities, often do what everyone else is doing.

Heritage. Maintaining a connection to where we come from is important to many people, especially in the United States or other former colonies. Whether someone's ancestors arrived in a place voluntarily or via human trafficking and abuse, it could be important for a person to explore their personal ancestry when selecting who to worship. My only word of caution is to ensure that you approach this mindfully.[2]

Activity. This is exactly what it sounds like. You know what you like, what you do for work and hobbies, and who you want to be. You find Gods who have well-documented aspects in one or more of those areas and decide to worship them. Most people who worship Gods use this as a criterion for selecting someone to worship, at least in the beginning.

Astrology. In astrological systems, specific Gods are associated with specific signs of the Zodiac. These deities may shift slightly based on the system a writer is using. Sometimes,

---

[2]Especially for those of us with various European ancestries and ethnic backgrounds, a "return to the roots" can be co-opted by the far-right. Anyone can worship the Gods. Far-right rhetoric relies on exploiting feelings of disempowerment and rootlessness, and it is important to resist it. You are worshipping the Gods you worship for your reasons, and others have their own — everyone has a perspective to offer, regardless of an individual's cultural heritage and/or ancestry. Developing a practice for the Gods, being committed to learning, and approaching the practice with reverence are what matters. Let your own thing be about repair without making it creepy, and avoid groups that don't allow people of all races and ethnic backgrounds in. In groups, what matters is respect for the Gods and coming together in service for them and one another.

the position of the rising sign or which sign the moon is in matter just as much as one's sun sign. You can explore this with some Google searches on Gods for specific signs. Keep in mind that "astrology" is a very general term, so you will see results for Western, Vedic, East Asian, and other forms of astrology. Speaking Platonically, the soul accumulates various traits (or garments) as it descends into the world of becoming, and the positions of the stars at birth have sometimes been used as signals of which Gods will be particularly prominent for a person that lifetime, although that is not the only thing that matters. Some astrologers believe that the planets *are* the Gods. While the planets are sacred to the Gods, even if a planet is associated with a God, the God transcends that planetary association.

Divination-based. Sometimes, especially in African Diaspora religions, the God(s) someone should worship closely are determined in divination. Divination protocols for such rituals are usually very intricate, and they require study and care for the practitioner to do them well. This book is not about those traditions, and if you are curious about them, I encourage you to do research on the ones that interest you, ideally learning from actual practitioners and leaders in those traditions. Outside of those specific religious contexts, someone could consult with divination specialists about deities. "Divination" is a broad category that encompasses far more than tarot and oracle cards, and it's not just about predicting the future! Often, people use divination to seek advice on something that has been bothering them or gain insights into circumstances they are facing so they can make informed choices. Divination of any kind is ideally conducted in a manner that connects with the Gods via prayers, offerings, and so on.

Experience. In Proclus' surviving hymns to the Gods, he makes frequent references to holy words of the wise that excite the soul towards the Gods. This divine bliss state sometimes literally happens to people. Very rarely, you're reading something, you have a dream, or a freaky chance occurrence hits, and it sends chills down your spine. It could even send the world topsy-turvy for a few hours or days. Something feels *right* about it. You may know the name of the God, or you may just know vague things about your experience and put the pieces together later on. It's a gift when this happens. As a word of caution, keep an eye on your mental health — brain conditions can mimic spiritual experiences, so practice self-awareness and be sure to follow up with a doctor if you suspect[3] that something is wrong. Intense bliss-state experiences will dissipate after a few hours or days, perhaps with some short-term aftereffects like an increased ability to enter a meditative state or a re-evaluation of your life goals. And they don't happen every day! "Smaller" experiences are more common — praying for a dream or an unambiguous sign is something people have done for millennia in pursuit of some milder spiritual insights.

---

[3]Generally speaking, "you are the chosen one" is something that only happens in Hollywood movies and messianic fringe groups.

3.1.1 An Example of Choice

When I was a teenager, I decided on Apollon and the Muses because I felt that poetry was the only thing I was good at. In the American cultural reception of Apollon, he is often taken to be synonymous with music and poetry. Little did I know that, when I made that choice, things would change and expand out from there — Apollon is a harmonizing God, first revealed in the truth-bearing triad in Platonism before weaving his way through various levels of emanation from the One. I was worried when I started studying library science that I still thought of him as my God when my work had nothing to do with him, and I struggled to find ways to relate my life to what I knew about him from his epithets, what scholars had written, and the things I saw people post online about worshipping him.

For several years, I strayed away and primarily worshipped Hermes, with Athene secondary, because they are very professionally relevant to my daily work. This was naïve of me given what I know now, and as soon as I was ready to know more about Apollon, specific things in my life fell into place that landed me back worshipping him daily — everything I needed to know was rooted in the Platonists. I worship Hermes much less now, but still in a professional capacity. We're human. How we pray, and who we pray to, evolves over time.

3.1.2 What About Specific Traditions?

The Soul's Inner Statues is a book about worshipping Gods at home, not about any specific religious tradition. Many of my examples draw on the Hellenic Gods because I have worshipped them for so long.[4] As a follower of Plato, I also firmly believe that it is important for avoiding cultural appropriation that Platonists engage with the Gods of the tradition. (Even for Platonists who worship other Gods, a moderate engagement with Hellenic myth and context is important for doing Platonic contemplation related to the primary Gods one *does* worship, regardless of where those Gods are from.) Specific religious traditions often have guidelines that are used to help devotees select a deity ... if the tradition doesn't just choose the God for them. What happens in those traditions usually falls into one of the categories that I have named above.

Some marginalized groups are very protective of their ancestral practices, usually due to outsiders exploiting and selling their practices for the outsiders' own financial and social gain and due to centuries of oppression and persecution from missionaries and state-sanctioned religious violence. Be mindful of this and seek to understand where others are coming from. Worshipping a God privately at home does not grant you automatic acceptance by the survivors of cultural genocide or conquest. Showing respect for their communities, being willing to learn, and committing to treating their traditions as sacred and not as commodities may go a long way, but then again, it may not. The decision is theirs.

---

[4]In my own non-Greek context; if you're interested in something connected to Greek methods of worship, I encourage you to connect with Greeks.

3.1.3 What About Being Chosen?

While I do believe in spiritual experiences, I *don't* believe that being "chosen" by a God is possible. What I *do* believe is that many (or is it just us Americans?) use vocabulary from pop culture fantasy novels and Christianity because we don't quite know how to put what we have experienced into words.

When people are saying this genuinely and not deceptively, I believe this means that they experienced the spiritual version of "friendship at first sight."[5] They saw a depiction of a God or started to learn about them and just *knew* they needed to worship that God. It can be a very magnetic pull and generate intense, difficult-to-describe emotions. The person making this claim is still the agent. They are the one who decides to offer the libation or light the incense. There can be spookier versions of this, such as jarring coincidences or dreams that always seem to point to the God; in those cases, our guardian spirit is likely trying to get our attention and let us know that worshipping this God may be fulfilling for us. It's still not chosenness.

Sometimes, people will describe their spiritual life as a *calling,* a term that is highly associated with Great Awakenings and evangelical Christianity in America, but which has since been secularized. It's now frequently used in America to describe people who give everything they have to their jobs because the job gives them meaning. *Calling* or *called* are simply culturally-specific words to describe that feeling of being excited about something, empowered to grow, and connected to something greater than oneself. I do not use this language.

---

[5]This is a real thing in friendship research.

In our multicultural society, it can lead to misunderstandings when someone doesn't have tacit cultural knowledge of the term's origins and context.

Related to this, one will sometimes hear the term *working with [deity]* instead of *worshipping [deity]*. Some of this usage comes from magical practices, and the modern occult movement's history is too out-of-scope to briefly trace why that usage is present. Beyond that, one will occasionally hear someone express that their upbringing in a conservative (usually Christian) sect has made them anxious about the term *worship* due to the traumatic experience. *Working with* can make the Gods seem more approachable. However, *worship* is the preferred term, even in cases when someone is doing a specific type of work, volunteer effort, or hobby to fulfill a vow made to a God. Our nature is not the same as the Gods — our role in the world is to be present to what is happening around us in the material world and to grow and change under their watchful guidance. We have agency and dignity, yes. The rites we perform, the meditations we do, and the other spiritual acts we train ourselves to do are all done to increase our harmoniousness with their providential power. They are the conductors; we are members of the orchestra.

3.1.4 What About Transformative Experiences?

Transformative experiences of the Gods are beautiful things. These can come in the form of dreams, experiences in journey meditations, sudden illumination from wisdom tradition texts, or even an awakening to divine beauty when we see the way the sun strikes newly-opened spring flowers. In ritual, it is not unheard of for someone to be overcome with strong feelings of connection and love when praying to a God for the first time, as if a floodgate has opened. Prayers can lead to steady streams of coincidences. Divination outcomes can teach us about the parts of ourselves we need to grow or let go of, and the techniques themselves put us in contact with the God(s) to whom we have consecrated our tools.

While it is not chosenness, a deep experience might indicate your *closeness* to a God, especially if you have been praying for guidance about the best God to devote yourself to or something similar. In Platonism, the Gods have something called *providential love* (eros pronoetikos) for us — a type of care flowing without cease and without boundaries to all who are open to receiving it. Experiencing bliss or a sense of deep connection in prayer can sometimes be mistaken for chosenness or some kind of special status. Having a religious experience, cleaning oneself up, and committing to excellence can also sometimes lean on the idea of being chosen as a self-soothing mechanism — we like to believe that someone else is rooting for us *specifically*, and it's useful to unpack why we may believe that is the case. Maybe we actually just chose a life (go us!) where we will do a specific set of activities, and a spiritual experience was the jolt that motivated us to finally get done what we had already committed to doing. The Gods are like the sun: our experiences of their rays depend on everything from weather to time of day to whether we have positioned ourselves somewhere we can be appropriately warmed.

The reason for emphasizing dangers is that we are all capable of self-deception, especially those of us who grew up in difficult environments. *After the Ecstasy, the Laundry* by Jack Kornfield describes the opportunities and pitfalls for people from a variety of religious and spiritual traditions who have experienced a sudden awakening. The biggest pitfall, according to him and others, is thinking that it's one-and-done and that we don't need to do work afterward (Kornfield, 2001). In the United States, many people have used visions of deities to prop themselves up as New Age cult leaders. Others have founded well-intentioned spiritual communities without any training — and it goes badly. Some have used a spiritual experience to quit working on themselves when they still have years of their life to live. Some engage in appropriation, spiritual materialism, and spiritual bypassing and transform the wonderful gift that was given to them by the Gods into something that causes pain and harm to others.

If a deep spiritual experience happens, approach it with humility. Take notes, do what you need to do, and follow up on your commitments. Decompress however you need. Continue to pray and explore your spiritual practice. Again, the practice evolves over time, as we are embodied souls moving through time. Learn from it.

3.1.5 An Important Caveat About Gods' Functional Roles

Many of us are initially drawn to a deity because they have a specific functional role. It establishes rapport between you and the God before you have first prayed to them, much like how reading a social media profile and learning that you have something in common with someone will prime you to treat them charitably, at least at first.

Often, someone may ask, "So, if I have x issue, which deity should I go to?" after they already have a foundational Gods-oriented outlook and household shrine. We are conditioned by the media to oversimplify what *divine epithets* and *spheres of influence* of a deity mean.[6] Aphrodite is *only* a Goddess of Love, for example, or Eir is *only* a Goddess of Healing, according to that mindset. We are now living in an era when much of the world is alienated from Gods, and yet this is also a time with tremendous cultural transmission, diffusion, and power for change. We must learn how to see Gods in a more holistic and less utilitarian/functional way.

Starting out with the traditional symbols, images, and epithets can assist you with creating a vibe in your space that will resonate with the God and deepen the link between you and them. Once we get to know a deity, however, these functional areas start to break down, and the God expands to encompass more and more of one's life. Apollon is most associated with poetry, music, light, and harmony, and yet I might pray to him for assistance with a family issue. I have worshipped Apollon for decades and can easily access that "I am praying to Apollon now" headspace. This deep familiarity facilitates connection even when moving into uncharted zones. When I started worshipping the Norse Goddess Eir, I understood her as a healing Goddess similar to Hygieia and Asklepios, but I now understand her as a Goddess related to healing, purifica-

---

[6]Again, an epithet is like "Apollon the Far-Shooter" or "Apollon the Harmonizer of All" or "Apollon of Delphi" — it marks some specific aspect of a God, and people will often use epithets to praise a deity when starting out a prayer.

tion, and the actions we do here in the material world due to her activity on the battlefield as a medic and the symbolism of her coming down from the mountain where the healing Goddesses do their craft — a battlefield is a symbol of embodiment in Platonism, and generation is seen as a type of warfare. I now include her in my purification prayers. This fusion is far less traditional, but it is personally meaningful, and it is the sort of thing that happens naturally as we unfold our relationship with a God through devotional acts. More traditionally, every place where a God has historically been worshipped will have its own unique take on what that God means (or meant) to the inhabitants, with specialized rituals, iconography, and other elements. The different ways in which we worship the same God are similar to dialects of a language. In cultures that have had more myths recorded, many of the mythic cycles have multiple variants, too.

In the Platonic tradition, every God is the totality of everything ("all in all") while preserving their own unique individuality and oneness. Gods "flow" into conversation with cultures or groups to produce unique fingerprints of how Gods operate in specific places. These "flows" impact their iconography, the items offered, the myths a people creates, how we see the God's sex and gender role[7], and so on. A group may even be

---

[7]We project these stereotypes onto the Gods based on how humans have given social meaning to human reproductive roles and functions — historically an important part of our societies, but less so in many American cultures nowadays. Gods who seem more active in generation and growth and care are often feminized, and Gods who seem authoritative or causal are often masculinized. Thus, Frigg, Hathor, Sunna, and Nantosuelta are Goddessess; Vulcan, Helios, Zao Shen, and Mani are Gods. The "fit" is never perfect — just as with humans — because nobody reflects all of the stereotypes. We can see this acutely with Goddesses like Athene and Artemis

united by a similar view of a God when they live very far apart
as long as they share a common outlook on life. These relationships between groups and the Gods evolve, progressing
forward in time.

Syrianus, in critiquing Aristotle's *Metaphysics*, Books 13-14,
wrote:

> [T]he whole placing of the stars involves much
> supposition on our part. Thus it is that the fixed
> stars are arranged in one way according to the
> Egyptians, but according to the Chaldaeans or the
> Greeks in another way (Syrianus, 2007: 191, 23–
> 25).

Gods do not have positions in the sky, but a similar idea applies here. When we create practices surrounding the Gods,
and especially when those practices become traditions and
influential cultural movements, we are arranging the Gods

---

who are masculinized, even though Athene presides over women's labor
production and Artemis was once involved in maturation rites for girls
and brides — or Gods like Dionysos and Apollon who are feminized while
simultaneously having their masculinity stressed through (for Dionysos)
connections to phallic worship and (for Apollon) connections in the ancient
world to older boys' adulthood rites. In many cultures, there are also Gods
who symbolically hold the potential of all reproduction, like Phanes, who is
depicted as gynandrous. Some types of symbolism remain important due
to their theurgic function and relationship to birth-death-rebirth cycles in
nature and mystery traditions, whereas others are less translatable across
time, place, and culture.

(For any Platonists reading this, the landmine of misconceptions about how
these topics intersect with the simplicty of the Henads and their "unfolding"
through the levels of the hypostases is similar to how the One, the Two, and
the Three mean something different at levels of emanation from the first
principle that are less proximate to matter; many people make an error
here similar to the one that Aristotle makes while critiquing the Forms in
his *Metaphysics*, and Syrianus' refutation is very relevant here.)

into structures based on what we come to know about them. Each of our practices may divide up the sky differently and omit some types of stories and deities in favor of others, but the same *potentiality* of divine multitude underlies all of this.

Sometimes, the functional role a deity has traditionally occupied is very important to us long after we've solidified who we worship the most. I have a soft spot for solar and light-related deities, and that comes out in my practice even though I know that these Gods cannot be reduced to the material sun.

3.2   A Chain, Unbroken

In Platonism, there is one other type of divine relationship — something that is not a choice and could never be a choice. In the Platonic tradition, every soul is in the *series* of a specific God. A *series* is a chain that begins with the God. It progresses through several levels of intermediary spirits, and the chain ultimately ends with us.

As incarnating souls, we "dip down" into various types of lives, from rational lives (think humans, orcas, or elephants) to nonrational lives (think incarnating as a cat). Above us are heroes, who have a dipping point of rational lives (so, they can't become cats), above them daimons and angels (who do not have dipping points into material bodies, unless one posits that some daimons dip into planets and stars), and finally, the Gods themselves. Every God has a chain of these intermediaries. At the risk of sounding too spatial for something that is not demarcated by space, the God is the "trunk," the angels are the "boughs," and the various levels of daimons are the branches that we (nodes that produce fleeting leaves) are suspended from. Each daimon has a cluster of souls it supervises. In addition, specific lives we choose have presiding daimons.

Because being in some God's series is an innate property of every soul, it is not special; because we are each individuals who express that individuality differently, every soul has its unique, particular way in which it is linked to the God that seeds it. This doctrine calls those of us who hold it to probe the paradox of something as ordinary as grass being so individually important.

Each soul only has *one* leader-God because its anchor point must be a unity; if the soul had many, it would not be a one. Platonism has its roots in the Ancient Mediterranean (and Greece specifically), but the leader-God does not need to be Greek — even in Late Antiquity, there were Platonic philosophers and Platonizing individuals from other polytheistic religious traditions. It is also a misconception that these Gods are limited to the twelve (or eleven, rather, because Hestia abides) discussed in Plato's *Phaedrus*. Both Proclus[8] and Hermias[9] push back

---

[8]"[Plato] defines according to the measure of the dodecad all the liberated Gods, though the multitude of them is incomprehensible, and not to be numbered by human conceptions; and though none of those theologists that have written any thing concerning them, have been able to define their whole number, in the same manner as they have the ruling multitude or the multitude of the intellectual or intelligible Gods. Plato however, apprehended that the number of the dodecad is adapted to the liberated Gods, as being all-perfect, composed from the first numbers, and completed from things perfect; and he comprehends in this measure all the progressions of these Gods." (Proclus, 1995:Book 6, Ch. 18, 85.7–16)

[9]Plato "said in the Timaeus that the Demiurge assigned the souls to gods on the basis of kinship (*okeiotês*), saying that 'he sowed some in the earth, some in the sun'. Here he has also talked about the nine types of life (*bios*) and also talked about the twelve gods, symbolically including the whole multitude [of them]" (Hermias, 2022: 197, 7–11), brackets from the

against this idea, and Damascius mentions individual souls who are in the series of the Gods of Tartarus in his *Phaedo* commentary at §540. The core thing to pull away from the concept of leader-Gods is something from Hermias:

> For this is the soul's happiness: to be able to imitate
> its own god, to the extent of each person's power,
> so long as [that person] lives life here [on earth] in
> an uncorrupted manner (Hermias, 2022: 198, 30).

Here, "uncorrupted" is hinting at what we will be discussing in the chapter on virtue about applying measure and mindfulness to our lives so we are not completely caught up in appetites and emotions. Imitation of our leader-God does not mean imitating myths; it means contemplating who the God is and how their blessings are distributed among all of us. For Apollon, it may mean focusing on goals related to harmonization and bringing multitudes back to unity in a variety of contexts; for Brigid, it may be embracing a lifestyle where making/creating and giving back to the community are core emphases.

Proclus, who is very verbose about the topic of leader-Gods, discusses what it is like when someone has that inner knowing and can align their goals with this sense of sameness and identification with one's leader-God.

> Even amid matters that seem difficult to under-
> stand or puzzling, the person who simply *knows*
> takes the easy path to divine understanding (*gnô-*
> *sis*) — retracing [a path that runs via] the divinely

translators.

inspired cognition (*entheos noêsis*) through which things become clear and familiar (*gnôrimos*), for all things are in the gods. The one who has antecedently comprehended all things is able to fill others with his own understanding. This is precisely what Timaeus has done here when he refers us to the authority of the Theologians and the generation of the gods celebrated by them.

Who, then, are these people and what is the understanding (*gnôsis*) that belongs to them? Well, in the first place, they are 'offspring of the gods' and 'clearly know their own parents.' They are offspring and children of the gods in as much as they conserve the form of the god who presides over them through their current way of life, for Apollonian souls are called 'offspring and children of Apollo' when they choose a life that is prophetic or dedicated to mystic rites (*telestikos bios*). These souls are called 'children' of Apollo to the extent that they belong to this god in particular and are adapted to that series down here. By contrast, they are called offspring of Apollo because their present lifestyle displays them as such. All souls are therefore children of god, but not all of them have *recognised* the gods whose children they are. Those who recognise [their leading gods] and choose a similar life are called 'children of gods.' This is why Plato added the words 'as they say,' for these souls [sc. those of the people to whose authority

Timaeus proposes to defer] reveal the order from
which they come — as in the case of the Sibyl who
delivered oracles from the moment of her birth
or Heracles who appeared at his birth together
with Demiurgic symbols. When souls of this sort
revert upon their parents, they are filled by them
with divinely inspired cognition *(entheos noêsis)*.
Their understanding *(gnôsis)* is a matter of divine
possession since they are connected to the god
through the divine light and [this sort of under-
standing] transcends all other [kinds of] understanding — both that achieved through [reasoning
through] what is likely *(di' eikotôn)*, as well as that
which is demonstrative *(apodeiktikos)*. The former
deals with nature and the universals that are in
the particulars, while the latter deals with incorpo-
real essence *(ousia)* and things that are objects of
knowledge. But divinely inspired understanding
alone is connected to the gods themselves (Proclus,
2013: 159.14–160.12).[10]

The description may sound utopian, as if no strife or suffering happens when someone knows their presiding God.
Importantly, we are still living in the material world, where
everything is separated out in space and time and things occasionally come into conflict with one another. Knowing one's
presiding God is more about having an inner sense of connection, agency, and empowerment in the face of these external
challenges than it is about having no conflict. An inner sense

---

[10] All soft and hard brackets from the translators.

of groundedness and belonging makes people more effective at handling their external situation, though.

Most of us have a lot of noise inside, and it takes a journey to figure out who that presiding God is. When it comes to embodiment, we have a big challenge: our forgetfulness and our ability to get hyper-preoccupied with what happens in specific incarnations or a series of incarnations. We sometimes pick life-patterns that align with our leader-God, and sometimes we don't. This is one of the reasons I called each of us unique — we make traces in the realm of coming-to-be like fingerprints. Some of our journeys express the tragic beauty of our leader-Gods, or the violent and horrific ones, or the depths of disappointment; others skim the surface of generation, like a bird of prey diving into the sea to come back with sustaining nourishment. The story of Cassandra, for instance, is metaphorically about having that deep insight, wanting something else, and then turning away from a God who cannot be run from because he is already the core of her; there are just as many people given the same prophetic gifts and who are not believed, yet never turn from the source of their good.

In this context, part of the maxim γνῶθι σεαυτόν (know thyself) is that we must strive to uncover this knowledge of who we truly are when we cast away all of those garments, and we must learn how to perform our current role in the most just way possible. This will not be easy regardless of how we make that approach.

Series has both the technical meaning just described and a secondary, slippery one, and in its slippery sense, it refers to the God or Gods who preside over our current lifetimes, who may or may not be the same as the God we are suspended from, and Gods who are highly related to specific talents and skills that we have in this lifetime. In other words, it can be tough to figure out who our leader-God is if we approach the problem solely based on what we're good at or the specific aspects of our daily grind.

> But we should ask which of the aforementioned six types of essential daimons they say is allotted to each person. Well then, they say that those who live according to their own essence (*kat'ousian*) – that is, as they were born to live (*pephukasi*) – have the divine daimon allotted to them, and for this reason we can see that these people are held in high esteem in whatever walk of life they pursue (*epitêdeuein*). Now [to live] 'according to essence' is to choose the life that befits the chain from which one is suspended: for example, [to live] the military life, if [one is suspended] from the [chain] of Ares; or the life of words and ideas (*logikos*), if from that of Hermes; or the healing or prophetic life, if from that of Apollo; or quite simply, as was said earlier, to live just as one was born to live.

> But if someone sets before himself a life that is not according to his essence, but some other life that differs from this, and focuses in his undertakings on someone else's work — they say that the intellective (*noêros*) [daimon] is allotted to this person, and for this reason, because he is doing

> someone else's work, he fails to hit the mark in
> some [instances] (Olympiodorus, 2015: 20.4–15).[11]

This confusion is not even a bad thing. In Ancient Greek art, there are beautiful scenes of Gods pouring libations to other Gods (Gaifman, 2018). Water is, among other things, a symbol of generation. We could view our incarnations that are lived away from our leader-Gods as libations, or gifts, for the other Gods — it is a system of mutual honor. A God pouring a libation for another God, or doing sacrifice in general for another God, is a gift of participation in a portion of their divinity to another, mediated by this weird realm of generation where so many things are possible. We are each, at our core, a one, and the flower at the core of us is always connected to the God we are suspended from; we are, at our periphery, dazzled by and participating in the amalgam of divine delights, a reflection in water of the feast that the Gods share in the *Phaedrus*. The Gods have no jealousy among them.

In generation, the beautiful divine patterns — each driven by a specific God — "freeze" out. Like a frustrated spin glass, there is no configuration of the whole system that can be utterly stable.[12] These conditions, and these phases of imperfect stability, evolve with time. We are locked in one position only to shift to another. We have that stability of who we are, but also the instability inherent to this environment. Some types

---

[11]All brackets from the translator.

[12]Spin glass is made of charged particles, with north and south poles. As with other magnets, they want to align north with south poles, but the configuration of the system prevents them from attaining that — shifting positions keeps putting them in conflict with yet another neighbor. Proclus describes this frustration in a different way in an essay on evils (Proclus, 2003).

of closeness with a God or Gods are driven by where we are in our life or lives; others are metastable over long periods; and only one relationship is absolutely intrinsic.

For those of us who hold that we belong to a God, we can add so much insecurity to this innate wonder of existence. Always focus on the God and be willing to evolve in how you relate to them. When we focus on the basics of prayer, ritual, and piety, we embrace the changing rhythms of our lives, which is in our nature as souls who are living a life in the material world. We allow ourselves to explore what our relationships to specific Gods mean without grasping tightly at something that will eventually fall away like sand through our fingertips.

In the last chapter, when I quoted from Plotinus before presenting the meditation exercise to you, there is a moment when Plotinus instructs us to ask for the God to come. This is the kind of contemplative practice that can guide you to who that leader-God is, if this practical Platonic section piques your interest. Repeat the meditation, or something similar to it, regularly over time, in conjunction with prayer. If you come into a state of frustration, wanting and desiring a definitive outcome or sign, sit with that feeling. Frustration often makes what we are frustrated about harder to accomplish. Check back in with the questions at the end of the Today Is Not Yesterday section of Foundations and the How Do You Pick A God methods and think about how to apply those.

If this does interest you, I end this section with these words: Close your eyes, find that stillness, and the God who is intrinsic to you is there. This is not something available to the privileged few, but directly accessible to all. Every human soul, and I do mean each and every one of us, is a prayer *continuously* without even realizing it, just as a heliotrope follows the sun.

3.3   Appropriation, Appreciation, and Cultural Reception

The term "cultural appropriation" may already have your stomach tightening, but don't worry: I am not going to tell you that you cannot worship a deity or set of deities. What I *am* going to say is that we all need to be aware of what, for lack of a better way of putting it, has been an extremely f—ed up past several hundred years. Appropriation is a way of discussing that power differential and the ways in which dehumanization and prejudice impact relations among people to this very day, especially where these relationships intersect with cultural "objects"[13] and practices.

Talking about appropriation doesn't always mean that you have to give something up — sometimes, it means adding to what you do so you can ensure it is more sensitive and respects others. When we worship a God, we want to know that we're doing it in a way that is ethical and grounded in a sensible response to our desire to worship them. We do not want to worship with a spirit of cultural voyeurism or contribute to contemporary problems of de-sacralization and

---

[13]I am using quotation marks here because these items, and the Gods they honor, are seen as commodities that can be bought and sold in the spirituality industry. They are not given the respect due to what is sacred.

commodification of the sacred. This section uses the positive frame that *we all want to be respectful devotees*.

I have done cultural appropriation in the past. In my 20s, when worshipping Hellenic Gods, I participated in non-Greek communities that saw themselves as cultural continuations of Ancient Greek religious practices. It's embarrassing to admit in writing, especially now that I realize how antagonistic many of those groups were to modern Greek/Hellenic organizations (based in Greece and the Greek diaspora) doing the same revivalist practices for Hellenic Gods. The truth is that I am an American without Greek ancestry, and while the Greek Gods and thematic motifs inspired by them have been part of American literature, art, and other cultural objects for centuries, our connection to these Gods is its own thing driven by *our* culture, not *theirs*. That is not bad or something worthless to be swept aside! We can look to what inspired creatives in the English-speaking world about specific Gods, myths, and stories, and we can do that without fetishizing a past that isn't ours to take and without a toxic pursuit of the "authentic."[14] (The same goes for Americans interested in Vikings or ancient Germanic tribes or Egypt. Know where you're coming from!) Some aspects of a transmission can be awful. To continue with this personal example, bad aspects of the cultural transmission from Greece include the pilfering of Greek cultural artifacts after the Greek liberation from the Ottoman Empire, the way in which Greek heritage was taken to prop up white

---

[14]For a fair treatment, I recommend reading this essay by a Greek graduate student, Katerina Apokatanidis (2021) about her experiences of othering in professional Classics: https://everydayorientalism.wordpress.com/2021/04/27/when-greece-is-not-ancient-colonialism-eurocentrism-and-classics/

supremacy while denigrating modern Greeks as too "ethnic" because they failed to fit that narrative, and the callous humanitarian tragedy that happened when Western European powers failed to intervene in the Greek Genocide because we were hungry for trade with the Ottoman Empire's successor state. I can worship these Gods, but I need to ensure that I am speaking from my own context and that I am doing what I can about the bad things — activities like supporting repatriation efforts and ensuring that I am mindful of modern Hellenes' continuity with their past.

This is where we move into "appreciation": Behaving respectfully and aligning as much as possible with what must be done in it. To use another example, for decades, yoga has been sanitized to make it more palatable for a white, culturally Christian audience. South Asian Americans in yoga like Anusha Wijeyakumar are advocating for more cultural sensitivity and awareness. One element of that is actually diving *deeper* into yoga philosophy and adopting the actual *lifestyle* of yoga. Another element is learning about its Gods, like Shiva, and their importance to the practice. If you do yoga, investigating Gods associated with it (and ways to honor them) and engaging with South Asian teachers is a great way to move from appropriation to appreciation. You can even start learning about the philosophy! I promise, as a follower of Plato, I won't judge you for being in a rival school! Stoicism, which is appropriated by modern society as a self-help tool, also has Gods at its core (okay, a lot of Zeus), and it should be approached in a holistic and respectful way, too. And Platonism has many Gods! The Muses, Athene, Apollon, Hermes, Zeus,

Rhea, Hekate, and a few others are very important to the tradition. Only recently did scholars start to take that seriously as an intrinsic aspect of the system.

At its most basic, be respectful of Gods and spiritual practices. Those of us who are learning about something as outsiders need to understand and embrace our outsider status for what it is. Two things I've found helpful to read are an article in the *Atlantic*[15] about how to mindfully and respectfully approach other cultures and a piece on cultural appropriation from *A Beautiful Resistance*[16] that discusses how appropriation is related to the treatment of everything as if it is a commodity item (Avins and Quartz, 2015; Wildermuth, 2021).

Those of us who worship Gods of a culture we're not from likely came across those deities through cultural reception. Cultural reception, the way I am defining it, refers to how something that originated from elsewhere is received and interpreted by a culture, and especially to how the receiving culture processes its relationship to that thing. For example, the cultural reception of ancient Mediterranean literature and philosophy in the English-speaking world has historically been tied to elite education, especially to white landholders and old money families. There is a further cultural reception at play nowadays in America where people who have historically had *less* access to the Classics are working with the material (as it was a privileged cultural corpus) and putting it in dialogue with other aspects of American culture. All of

---

[15]https://www.theatlantic.com/entertainment/archive/2015/10/the-dos-and-donts-of-cultural-appropriation/411292/

[16]https://abeautifulresistance.org/site/2021/6/03/plague-of-gods

us in America, colonizers and colonized, are swimming in that unique amalgam. Something similar is happening with Latin American countries' interest in their own histories of Classical reception, although I don't know the details beyond a press release for an initiative that came across my social media feed in 2020 or so.

People living in the daughter cultures of the ones that produced the ancient myths we're reading and reacting to in modern American culture may have very little knowledge about the role their ancient literature plays here, depending on how frequently (and deeply) they interact with us. Due to globalization and the Internet, there are many opportunities for this to create clashes — it's one thing to see a news story from halfway around the world about a new art installation of Medusa and quite another thing for someone to suddenly have a crash course in American politics in the Reddit comments about said installation. In a spiritual context, the way Wiccans relate to the Goddess Hekate is very different from how a Greek American community may worship her in Astoria, New York. They are two different traditions.

3.3.1   Syncretism and Eclecticism

Syncretism is what happens when you combine belief systems — and sometimes Gods — in a systematic way. To use a linguistic analogy, syncretism is a lot like what happens when speakers of multiple languages convene in a single location — at first, there are communication issues, but a way to communicate quickly starts. Eventually, a creole language is produced, with its own vocabulary, grammar, and syntax drawn from all of the components that fed into it. It's very different from speaking multiple languages (the analogy for practicing multiple ways of worship at the same time, but keeping them separate). At some point, the new language is formalized and becomes an institution of its own.

Syncretism is often contrasted with eclecticism. Many eclectics value the relationships with each specific God and are not worried about connecting the dots in a completely fused way like syncretics are. Eclectics may be characterized as people who don't care about systems at all, but this is rarely the case — people who respect Gods put care into how they are worshipped, but that care may take different forms depending on what someone prioritizes. It is all systematic! Eclectics are willing to tolerate ambiguity and juggle different systems; syncretics want to unite it into a whole. Most people are honestly somewhere in the middle, and others (like me) do not find this framing to be that helpful outside of theological writings. I tend to focus on whether or not a ritual framework is "all over the place" or coherent and how much respect is actually given to the Gods and the liturgical protocols. If something is not coherent or if it is disrespectful, it's not good.[17]

Syncretic and eclectic practices are what most of us in America will end up doing — and, if not us, our children. We

---

[17]I once attended a small Unitarian Universalist Church on the Sunday they were doing a Wiccan-style ritual. They did not observe the circle boundaries and chaotically combined the Chinese five elements with Celtic symbolism and deities and Tibetan singing bowls. The result was a chaotic mess. It would have needed appropriate observance of "cutting the circle" protocols (so many people had come in late and had just walked in and out during the observance!), purification protocols, and an audit of how the ritual elements were combined and whether it was too much to be respectful or appropriate — at minimum — in order to work.

come from many places, with a vast array of cultural inputs, and America is a melting pot. In addition, almost everything is Americanized (to some extent) eventually. What matters most is that we stay curious about the Gods and our practice. The world is full of Gods, as Thales said. Our relationship with the Gods changes over time, as the Platonists say, because we are alive in time.

An example of a syncretic (and slightly eclectic) practice would be if someone were to map hearth Goddesses from their heritage onto physical directions and pray to them according to direction at the beginning of each major ritual. Returning to what I said about worshipping many hearth Goddesses, I could hypothetically set Frigg as East/Air, Hestia as South/- Fire, Brigando as West/Water, and Nantosuelta as North/Earth. This would be a nesting doll of syncretism. First, I am looking at Goddesses from four different contexts; second, I am combining them with directional quarters that are used in modern popular Wicca; and third, I am praying to all of the Goddesses at the same time using that directional context. The unifying elements here would be that these Goddesses represent both hearth Goddesses of my maternal and paternal families, plus the Hellenic Gods that I pray to out of fondness. It would efficiently get around questions of who to pray to (and when) by praying to them all at once. This is not something that I actually do, but it is a thoughtful treatment that someone, somewhere, could respectfully do. The directions for the Goddesses are not set arbitrarily. Anyone visiting a ritual would need to be briefed on the context.

Another example of a syncretic practice would be the fusion of Belesama with Minerva in Roman Gaul. Belesama is a solar Goddess, with strong water associations; she is truth-bearing, good with words, and radiant. During that historical period, she was seen as the local version of Minerva by Roman authorities, and the worship of the two Goddesses fused together. Belesama and Minerva are distinct Goddesses. I would, based on personal contemplative experience, place Belesama in a similar conceptual space to Apollon, Aletheia, and Helios. Sulis, another Goddess who was syncretized by Romans to Minerva, was also worshipped as Minerva during the Roman occupation. She has more in common with Hygieia and Salus.

The understanding of deities as being similar is called *interpretatio*, a Roman word. It was used by the Romans to identify which local Gods of conquered peoples (or which Gods of a neighboring people) corresponded to specific Roman Gods, often for the purpose of integration into the Empire and cohesion. Importantly, even when names are equated, people would still swear oaths by their own Gods, and many people active in theology — like Iamblichus — were against the equation of names (Iamblichus, 2003; Parker, 2017). In many cases, even when etymologies are clear, a deity may not actually be the same. Mars and Ares, based on their iconography and how people worshipped them in antiquity, are definitely not the same! Nor are Eshu and Hermes despite the many commonalities they have as Gods who are associated with boundaries, playful trickery, and liminal spaces. We do not know the upper limit of the number of Gods. For this reason, even when it's easy to *conceptualize* a God by relating them to a God you already know a bit about, it's best to approach them as a distinct person unless something happens in ritual that makes it clear that they are the same. This is a very different approach from what happens in modern secular media when it *uses* mythology and deities. It is typically not being created by people with deep theological understanding of many Gods, but to sell stories based on myths that we have imported via cultural reception, and it is rarely coming from a place of respect.

The more you read about syncretism, eclecticism, and interpretatio, the more questions might arise. I advise you to worry less about this and more about cultivating your personal spiritual practice. To whom do you pray at home? Specific Gods … and perhaps the household spirits and ancestors. However, as you learn about the Gods you have chosen to worship, you may encounter writings, videos, and podcasts that conflate deities from neighboring cultures or sources that claim that all lunar Gods are the same. The information in this section will prepare you for that and will hopefully help you evaluate what you encounter.

3.4   Exercise: Do Some Research, Then Pray

Choose one (or more) of the methods listed above for selecting deities. Use resources available to you to do some searching. It's OK to go on Wikipedia — check the Talk page of whichever deity's page you land on if you see anything you're really unsure about. The Talk page can be accessed at a link just above the page title, and it shows you what editors have been arguing about while maintaining the page.

Other options include looking up terms like *Norse pantheon list of Gods* in Google. When you search, you will see a combination of how-to articles, blogs, Tumblr posts, academic articles and pages, and so on. As you shift among different resources, note the creator's perspective when writing the piece, especially differences between historical information and modern insights that arise from practice, political outlook, and other aspects of someone's personality, habits, and culture.

Narrow down to one or two deities. Do another search, but just for them. You might use *-tumblr -twitter -pinterest* to remove things from the results if you're using Google.

Here are a few questions to guide you:

- What kinds of offerings are typically given to this deity?

- What are their main symbols?

- Were they worshipped in any specific regions?

- What kinds of appearances does this God make in pop culture today?

- Are there any surviving ancient prayers that you could recite for them?

Once you have done your research, write down the God's name on a piece of paper and go to your small shrine space. After praying to the hearth Gods, pray to one of the Gods you have chosen. Greet them, say a few heartfelt words, and give an offering. The offering could be the same one that you gave to the hearth Gods or something based on your research.

If you know extemporaneous speaking isn't for you, you're welcome to prepare something written to read for the God during this first introductory prayer. You might give your name, the reason you are praying to this deity out of all of your other options, and provide some important information. What would you tell another person you've just met?

After praying, take a few moments to pause. Write some notes about the experience and do more prayers over the next few days.

The information you've learned about the God is also useful for contemplative practices.

Chapter 4

Purification

I pray after showering. For me, washing up and prayer are linked. Whenever I shower later in the day — for instance, if I've returned from the gym — I immediately think of the prayer beads at one of my shrines, even if I am also ravenous because I've worked up an appetite.

When I was just starting out with developing a solid prayer routine (after years of disorganized living during undergrad and grad school), this is how my mornings would go:

1. Wake up, feed cat, shower

2. Set the kettle on

3. Pray to Hestia and a God of the day, whom I selected at random

4. Upon the kettle ringing, I'd end the prayer and get ready for work

It was a simple routine — the kind of thing a young professional juggling many obligations and a chaotic mind could manage. New adulthood can be rough.

But why did I do the ritual after showering? I wanted to keep my purification practice as simple as possible.

Ritual purity can sound like a dour topic. The Gods are present everywhere, to everyone, and to everything, so why do we need to wash up if they're already here?

As discussed in earlier chapters, when we do a prayer ritual for the Gods, we are engaging with both them and a plethora of symbols and signs that point to them. Symbolically, doing a purification is a "stripping away" of material garments and the excesses that harm our focus. We approach the Gods clean, with ritual preparation designed to get us into a focused mindset.

What you do for purification is up to you. We are all different people, and depending on your habits, you may emphasize physical or mental purification — sometimes I can get anxious and scattered, which means that mental purification is important to me, but someone with an easier time there might place less emphasis on it. In this chapter, we will go over some common techniques for both, and then we will discuss what to do in special circumstances.

4.1   Physical Purity

When we acknowledge the presence of the Gods, especially ones whom we hold dear, we are welcoming fond associates into our awareness. Like inviting someone over, someone might shower, put on clean clothes, and the whole works. Another person could freshen up by washing hands, putting on deodorant, and tidying their hair. Writing after the pandemic, when so many more people are experiencing fatigue and related issues as Long COVID side effects, it's important to stress that you do what you can do. That said, you *should* shower before a structured shrine ritual[1] if you have just had sex, if you've returned from a funeral or memorial observance, or if you are getting over an illness that left you bedridden.

The Soul's Inner Statues is providing a generic practice, albeit one informed by the Platonists due to my bias. The principles in this chapter should give you a solid baseline for your household practice, regardless of who your hearth Goddess is and which Gods you chose to get to know in the last chapter, and regardless of your philosophical inklings.

Traditions that worship many Gods call for purifications in a variety of circumstances. If you decide to shift into a specific traditional practice due to fondness and inclination, you will learn techniques and protocols specific to that tradition. This usually happens during the onboarding and/or initiation practices, when you are taught what to do by a mentor or teacher.

During any purification, prayers or intentions may be voiced ("let me be pure", "with this water, I am pure," &c.) to mark the action as sacred, but that is not required. This list of general methods is not exhaustive, so I encourage you to look up detailed instructions on how to do one of these things if you need to. Use YouTube if you want to see some-

---

[1]An *unstructured* prayer is one in which you just take a few breaths and pray wherever you are. It doesn't always involve offerings; a *structured* ritual or prayer operates within the ritual framework you've set up. This isn't set-in-stone terminology, and the basic point is that you should feel free to pray informally at any time.

one demonstrate how to do it, and use text-based resources online if you want a step-by-step walkthrough of one. Keep in mind that there are many ways to do each of these, so you may want to compare and contrast videos and instructional outlines from a few people.

- **Smoke cleansing.** This is common in the United States nowadays. To do smoke cleansing, you light a bundle of herbs, extinguish it to embers, and wave the smoke around the area or person(s) you want to cleanse. Sage bundles are often available in stores; however, rosemary and other herbs can also be bundled and used for this purpose. Smoke cleansing may go by other names, like *recels*, in specific cultural traditions. Please note that smoke cleansing and smudging are different. Smudging, while it comes from a term used in English for any thick purifying smoke (often, according to the Oxford English Dictionary, to ward off insects), via lexical drift, it has come to be the preferred term for the burning of dried substances in several Native American cultures' ceremonies, and they have asked that others stop using the term for clarity.

- **Taking a shower, doing a ritual bath, or washing up.** This could be as simple as the morning shower you do before getting ready for work, a washing of the hands and face in the evening, or a fully-drawn bath. In some traditions, ritually sanctified water is poured over someone.

- **Salt water and herbs.** In this method, a dried fragrant plant bunch/twig/leaf (often rosemary or bay) is lit on fire and extinguished in saltwater immediately. This is then sprinkled on the person(s) participating in the prayer.

- **Salt water.** Salt is combined with water, and a prayer is said over the water to ask the Gods of purification to imbue it with cleansing power. Sometimes, the one creating the holy water asks for blessings from the sun or moon.

Remember that it is possible to modify any of the above purification techniques if need be. For any techniques that involve fire, please remember fire safety, as dried herbs can be brittle.

4.1.1 A Brief Word on the Underworld Gods and Ancestors

Depending on context, deities related to the underworld — and ancestors — may need to be worshipped separately. This is strictly the case in contexts with the Hellenic Gods, when it's important to *never* share a drink or food with underworld deities like Hades — they get all of it — and where the offering place to the underworld Gods is separate.

It's a best practice to Google how an underworld deity is meant to be worshipped before you do it. If, during your research, you learn that the deity you are worshipping has *strict* separation (like in the Hellenic example above), I recommend using separate libation vessels and receptacles. Some traditions will allow ancestors' photos to be placed at or near your usual household shrine; in others, it's best to keep any ancestor shrines separate. A few years ago, when researching whether I could have my ancestors at the same shrine as my ancestral household Gods, I learned that in many ritual liturgies for Norse Gods, ancestors are toasted in the same ritual as Gods, and many practitioners put them together on shrines.

"Separation" is relative. Use a low shelf or a place on the floor that you put up and take down as needed, removing the items to a box when not in use. One could use a wood yoga block as a floor table to hold the ritual items, a cutting board with raised feet (IKEA has one), or even the storage box (if it's sturdy enough). You could even convert a wall where you display dead family members' photographs to an ancestor area by simply adding a small console table and a place for a candle and flowers. It's advised to move photographs of the living elsewhere.

At my main household shrine, I pray to household Goddesses and ancestors during the final few days of the lunar calendar. At a small meditation table that is low to the ground, I have a shrine for underworld Gods: I worship the Erinyes, Hades, Persephone, Hel, and Erecura. If I didn't have a history of worshipping the Erinyes, I would just do a pop-up shrine for specific underworld Gods as needed at the end of the month and on special evenings, so don't take me as a model on this.

The waning moon into the dark moon is an excellent time to connect with underworld Gods and ancestors, as are times of your life when you are in mourning.

4.2 Mental Purity

Mental purification techniques are what can help center the mind and empower you to stay focused while doing ritual. It is simply *being able to focus on the ritual and on the God(s)* — nothing more, nothing less. Iamblichus, when describing Pythagorean precepts in the *Life of Pythagoras*, wrote, "In going to a temple, it is not proper to turn out of the way; for divinity should not be worshipped in a careless manner" (Iamblichus, 2020).

Sometimes, this comes easily. Sometimes, calming one's mind is like trying to soothe spooked horses.

There are times when I've imprudently checked email before my morning prayers and have been slammed with every awful thing in the world or a to-do list item that sets me into a panic. Or it can be a rainy day, or a day with horrible weather waiting for me, and I am already tense just looking outside and thinking of how on Earth I am going to get to work without slipping on ice. Rarely, arguments or bad life experiences can linger for days, even weeks. We all have things going on in our lives.

What I find useful during those charged days is to slow down. I try — sometimes unsuccessfully, but we're all works in progress — to avoid checking the news or my email before praying so I don't see things that make my stomach churn. I do a two-minute mindfulness meditation with an app to wind myself down.

It can be useful to have backup plans for when mental disquiet happens to you: Slowing down, you will not have as much time, which could stress you out even more if you haven't planned ahead. We all know that things will disrupt our schedules sometimes. Strategize for the inevitable — pick a mindfulness technique to use in times of duress, and plan out different lengths of your rituals.

Non-meditation mental purification techniques I recommend are:

- **Take a social media break.** Pick one or two days each week to uninstall and block all of your social media apps — it works best if the days are always the same. Ensure that anyone who absolutely needs to speak to you has your contact information, and plan on what you will do while disconnected. If you are very online, this will not feel pleasant due to the dopamine withdrawal, so plan a few more self-care activities than you think you need. If you have a tough time following through, when I was trying to reduce my Twitter usage during the pandemic lockdown, I found great success in changing my password and putting the only record of the new password beneath an icon of Athene.

- **Write out your to-do lists or do a thought dump.** This is especially useful for anyone who wakes up with a sudden awareness of everything that needs to happen that day. Use paper or your favorite app.

- **Have some self-care techniques handy.** These can be small things like doing a mud mask, a sequence of stretches, or diving into a folder you have of heartwarming letters from friends. You could also listen to chapters from a self-care audiobook. One book I've appreciated so far this year is *Pause, Rest, Be* by Octavia F. Raheem (Raheem, 2022).

- **Listen to music on an upbeat playlist, preferably without lyrics.** It's harder to get earworms when you're listening to instrumental music (and, speaking from experience, it can be very distracting to pray with a song stuck in one's head!), and music has such power to restore mood. You can find happy and upbeat playlists that feature jazz, classical, ambient, kora, or whichever genre you love.

- **Do grounding and centering.** This is the visualization technique mentioned several dozen pages ago, and you can find recordings on YouTube and in some meditation apps. Essentially, you visualize being connected to the Earth and Sky.

- **Get enough sleep.** Sleep power-washes your brain and makes you ready for the next day. Do what you need to do to get to bed earlier.

4.2.1   Exercise: Backup Rituals

This exercise builds on the idea of habit-bundling from previous chapters. Most of you are now worshipping the Gods in the morning or evening, with prayer added onto your other habits — like praying after you shower or after you brush your teeth.

Take out some post-it notes or pen and paper or open a digital whiteboard app like Mural. Depending on the time of day when you want to pray, write down what you tend to do at each step of your morning or evening for five scenarios:

1. You wake up late (or, for evening people, when you get home late).

2. You have lower energy than usual and need something simple.

3. You're traveling and are in a hotel or a guest in someone else's home.

4. People are visiting and you have to juggle hosting responsibilities.

5. You are experiencing high levels of stress or anxiety and need to focus on contemplative and de-stress techniques.

The ritual you've already been working on is your core ritual — the practice you can come back to as your "home base" when praying to Gods, daimons, and ancestors. Creating your backup rituals is an opportunity to embrace realism while maintaining connection.

Decide how much time you have for taking pause with the Gods in each of these scenarios. Thirty seconds? Two minutes? Five? Ten? Write down exactly what you will do and make sure your decisions are written out on notecards (or in an easily-accessed digital note-taking app) so you have them handy.

For the next four days, try each of the rituals. Make note of any adjustments.

- What feels satisfying?

- What is dissatisfying?

- Are you being realistic about the amount of time you have, the interruptions you may face, and elements of your life that always derail you when you're under pressure?

- If you're sleepy or groggy, should you really do that meditation?

- What is the bare minimum physical purification you can commit to doing?

If you travel frequently, this is also an opportunity to set up a travel kit. Mine is simple: I found a small jar and bowl at Goodwill. I bring prayer beads for several Gods, and I have wood bookmarks of Athene and Apollon that I put in place card holders (the wood name card holders that you may have seen at weddings on the table). If I'm in a hotel, I use that. If not in a hotel, I spend a few minutes with prayer beads. One time, while staying with an acquaintance in a small apartment that had very little privacy, I prayed using a set of beads in the brief few minutes they were in the shower.

4.3   The Kind of Consecration You Don't Want

There is a concept for something in Ancient Greek Religion, *agos* and *enagēs*, that is worth mentioning here — while the concepts are culturally specific, they describe something that I would argue is universal. It may even be very poignant and relevant for those of us living in places that suffered from intense violence in the past.

Conceptually, this term usually refers to someone doing something so wrong that it *consecrates them to a deity or divinity,* but in the worst way possible. The Gods are wholly Good, so they do not punish us. Behaviors that we engage in can, however, lead us down roads that will burn us because that is what is statistically likely and necessary in those circumstances. This term also has a *positive* sense in cases where it refers to the effect of swearing an oath — one swears by the God(s), and the action is consecrated to whichever God(s) were mentioned in the oath. This sets a boundary of necessity on one's behavior.

In the negative sense, the behavior that consecrates one to a God — and badly — is the inverse of what we will cover in the chapter on virtue. I once had a coworker who told me that she was a terrible person and that I wouldn't believe the things she'd done. I asked her if she had ever murdered or raped anyone, she said no, and that was the end of that. We often experience social shame and similar states as totalizing, catastrophic things. It is a growth process to learn to react appropriately to our own flaws. Most of us have not *personally* done truly terrible things.

I associate the negative necessity-driven consecration most strongly with the hostility of land spirits and the dead in places that have been the sites of genocide and similar blood crimes. For example, the Sullivan Campaign in Upstate New York massacred Native Americans to make more land available to Revolutionary War heroes, and the heinous act cannot be washed away. Among the Hellenic Gods, it's usually Goddesses called the Erinyes (Alekto, Tisiphone, and Megaira) who demand appeasement once blood crimes occur. The effects of this state cannot be washed away with a simple purification; instead, cleansing demands work. Those of us taking actions to make things better — even if what we can do is small — are far better off than people embracing the outcomes of unjust acts.

> But how is it reasonable for descendants to pay the penalty for [the sins of] their forebears? Well, chiefly [because] they have inherited their estates and their gold and silver, often acquired by wrongful means, which is enough for them to incur a penalty. And then too the souls of the forbears suffer along with those of the descendants that are having a difficult time [here below]. And they [*sc.* the descendants] do not suffer [these] punishments undeservedly, for the person who deserves to suffer such things is led into that kind of family, since providence and the divine nature and the gods who are the guides of fate transcendentally weave all things together in order and in accordance with justice (Hermias, 2018: 101, 10–20).[2]

Essentially, due to reincarnation, souls will choose the kinds of remedies they need to improve in their next life. Everyone who inherited difficult immoral legacies has the opportunity to improve things now. We were not put in this situation because we were bad people. We are in this situation because, when we chose this life, we trusted that we could come to do the right thing.

---

[2] All brackets are from the translators.

If you find yourself in this situation, do what you can, and make sure you're not taking the spotlight for simply being a decent person. There are many platforms trying to lure us to warp our efforts to help into content for our "audiences" to show what great people we are, and all the while ad revenue is rolling into the platform due to our engagement. It is equally easy to overextend ourselves due to the magnitude of human suffering and horrible behavior around us.

4.4   Guidelines for Purification in the Everyday

The guidelines below are ones that I am providing as suggestions for anyone praying to Gods. If you decide to pursue learning a specific tradition, you might find it has different protocols, and that's okay — just have something to ensure that you are making space for this. These are important symbols of the impermanence of life, and acknowledging them is like acknowledging the silence in a music score. Life is made of both the notes and the pauses.

- **Mourning.** Wait until the new moon to offer structured shrine rituals for non-underworld Gods. Cover shrines to non-ancestors and non-underworld Gods. You can still pray informally to any God, though. If a close relative dies, especially in the final few days of the lunar cycle, I recommend waiting a full lunar cycle and beginning again at the new moon after that. The night before you resume your ordinary prayer routine, put a photo of your new ancestor on the shrine where you keep ancestor-related items (or create a pop-up shrine) and do something meaningful for them.

- **Birth/adoption/fostering.** Take a bit of time (at least a few days) to settle in, and avoid most structured prayers and rituals during this time. After a few days (for adoptions/fostering) or weeks (make sure you're physically recovered enough from the birth process to exert yourself), everyone showers or washes up and puts on nice clothes. Introduce the new member of the family to the household Gods. Eat whatever foods you find special and offer some of them to the Gods. For babies, this can include a naming ceremony. Use one of your backup rituals for as long as you need.

- **Menstruation.** Be respectful if you are in a space where there are menstruant taboos (e.g., Kemetism, Hinduism), but otherwise, change your products before praying. Do not approach the shrine if you are experiencing debilitating pain. If you are in that much pain, you need to rest with a hot water bottle.

- **Sex.** Clean yourself up before you pray.

- **Sickness.**

  - If you are having an acute sickness, do not do structured shrine prayers if you cannot get up to do ordinary household things.

  - If you have a chronic illness and are having a flare-up, either refrain from your structured prayers or implement one of your backup rituals. I recommend thinking about your backup rituals in terms of having a low-energy prayer routine, medium-energy prayer routine, and high-energy prayer routine so your practice can fit the rhythm of the condition you are managing. It is OK if your lowest-energy routine is you in bed murmuring a mantra or favorite chant under your breath.

– If you are asymptomatic or mildly symptomatic and can do normal activities, try your full or low-energy backup ritual. If something doesn't feel right, focus on recovering. As mentioned in the bullet point above, there are ways to bring moments of reverence into your day without overextending yourself.

– During any sickness, you may pray to healing deities, either formally or informally, or ask that someone else do so on your behalf. Just please rest.

- **Extreme stress.** Focus on a backup ritual. Make sure you do whatever is in your emotional first aid kit.

4.5 Exercise: Pull It All Together

Do a brief meditation or grounding and centering exercise, then pray to a household God, ancestors, or one of the Gods you have picked after the previous chapter. See how taking pause impacted you. The next day, try a different type of purification exercise.

Do this for a few days while being mindful of the purification's impact on you. Pick the one or two options that seem to work best and stick with them. You can always revisit this if need be.

Chapter 5

Ritual Mechanics

Human lives are not the same from season to season, year to year, and decade to decade. The stars and planets trace out their many orbits. We change jobs. We marry. We achieve some things and fail at others. We die.

Everywhere around us, we see rhythms — personal, regional, global, celestial. In Proclus' *Timaeus* commentary, the philosopher points at the divine presence within things as seemingly intangible as time durations and motions of the heavens, and he names them Gods:

> There is, of course, a parallel with the sacred tradition which worships the former invisible [numbers] that are the causes of these [visible ones] by naming Night and Day as gods, as well as by delivering those things that commend one to the month and the year, the invocations and self-manifestations. These things are considered not as things to be totted up on one's fingers, but rather as among the

things that have divine subsistence — things which the sacred laws of those who serve as priests command us to worship and honour by means of statues and sacrifices. The oracles of Apollo also confirm this, as the stories say, and when these things were honoured, the benefits that result from the periods belonged to human beings, both the benefits of the seasons and those of other [periods] similarly. However, when these things were neglected a condition contrary to nature was the result for everything around the Earth. Not only that, but Plato himself in the *Laws* (X 899b2) positively shouts out that all these things are gods: seasons, months and years — just like the stars and the Sun. We are introducing no sort of innovation when we say that it is worthwhile to conceive of the invisible powers that are prior to these visible things [as gods]. So much for these matters Proclus, 2013: 89.15–37.[1]

Within our human lifetimes, there are times when we all pray for things we need or want in our lives: success at work, a new job, the satisfactory resolution of difficult interpersonal interactions, a better apartment, the ability to get to a flight on time. Whether we pray by venting about an issue and then asking for the best and most appropriate resolution possible (praying for what is good) or we actually ask for something specific (which has its benefits and risks), it's something every spiritual person does at some point or other.

We also pray according to seasons: when new herbs we

---

[1]All brackets belong to the translators.

are growing from seed first send up their shoots, when the ice and snow come and recede, for a gentle landfall of the hurricanes pummeling our shores during hurricane season. We pray for good harvests, happy new years, and abundant gift-giving seasons. Human beings pray about everything.

This chapter is about the mechanics of devotional activity. It provides guidance on how you can build on the spiritual habits that you have already been engaging in to set yourself up for long-term success. We will begin discussing the lunar and solar cycles, then get into specific types of cycles that happen in our lifetime — age milestones, deaths, and the inevitabilities of our lives. First, though, let's do a framing exercise.

5.1   Do What Is Achievable

Throughout this chapter, you may have ideas. These could be about the way you want to honor sacred temporal rhythms, be it through decorating your home, cooking special foods, or simply specific types of rituals you want to do. They may be about specific worship cycles you want to do for one or more deities. They could be about involving your kids.

Some things to keep in mind while reading are:

1. *Are other members of my household or roommate situation going to participate? Do I have anyone locally who does similar things and with whom I could collaborate on lunar holidays?*

2. *How much time do I have?* The civic calendar does not give us these days off. We spent much of the last chapter

designing our plans for success even in adverse situations, and the same thing applies here.

3. *How am I going to keep track of when to get things ready?*
   If you want to have flowers at the solstices or switch
   out wreaths, factor in shipping times when you set up
   your reminder system. I use Google Keep for reminders
   because the notifications on my phone contain useful
   information without too many irrelevant elements, and
   my solstice reminders are set for November 30 and May
   31 (about three weeks in advance). You can also set reminders in a system like Google Keep for your grocery
   list with a prompt to check whether any special days are
   coming up while you are planning your shopping.

4. *Which God(s) do I want to worship?* There are many deities
   who are related to the Sun, Moon, and seasonal cycles.
   The same "selecting deities" criteria apply here that applied to picking your first Gods to worship back in Foundations.

5. *What is my "special occasions" religious budget?* We all
   have different life situations, so (a) be realistic about
   what you can afford and (b) it's better to have less for
   special occasions, but have it come from a more ethical
   source, than to buy a large quantity of things from a
   less ethical one. The Gods do not care how much is in
   our paycheck or how many assets we have. The Gods
   need nothing. What matters is the symbolism and how
   it emphasizes our awareness of and connection to the
   Gods.

You can react to these questions in a notebook, a note on your phone, or something in your audio memo app. Practical work like this may seem like I am dragging sublime, transcendent activities through deep mud, but plans make all of the difference when you are having a hectic week at work, a bad few nights' sleep, &c. Speaking from personal experience, having a plan means the difference between decision paralysis (when we often end up doing nothing and feeling disappointed in ourselves) and actually meeting the demands of our messy lives (when we feel relieved that we know ourselves well enough to have cut ourselves some slack).

With your own life context now in mind, keep your notetaking tool handy and think of what makes sense for you.

Revisiting Time Blocking

This is a perfect time to revisit the time-blocking activity you did in Foundations (or start it if you haven't done it). Is it still working out for you? After reading this chapter, are there things you want to shift?

5.2 Following the Sun and Moon

The quotation from Proclus describes how the Gods are in everything around us. The most striking rhythms we see in our daily and monthly lives are the changes in the sky — the path of the moon and the sun's journey. Across cultures, the sun and moon are often crucial elements of a spiritual practice.

This section will provide some ideas for venerating them. It is not a comprehensive survey of solar or lunar worship, and I encourage you to make note of what sparks your curiosity. One noteworthy omission is the astrological rhythms of the sun, moon, and planets — some people who worship Gods focus on when the sun, moon, and other celestial bodies (sometimes even constellations) are in different astrological positions. Astrology is not part of my background, nor is ceremonial magic, so we will not focus on that here. However, *astronomy* is part of my background, and one of the best recently-published books about getting to know your local sky-rhythms is *Astronomical Mindfulness*. It will orient you to the sky where you live, and its activities and mindfulness prompts can be integrated into spiritual contemplation.

5.2.1 Venerating the Moon

There are four main types of lunar veneration: the rhythms of waxing and waning, moonrise, moonset, and eclipses. It is a rare person who venerates the moon in all of these ways — people who have that kind of time are, generally speaking, devoted to spiritual lives to an extent beyond what is attainable for most working adults. I do not follow moonrise and moonset, for example, nor do I follow the eclipses unless they happen when I am awake.

In many places, the moon is seen as a feminine symbol related to fertility and the process of generation. Writers have long pointed out the relationship between its cycle's length and the length of menstrual cycles. The waxing, full, waning, and new phases have often been mapped onto the luteal phase, ovulation, follicular phase, and menstrual phase, although the mappings vary. In other cultures, the moon and its local presiding God have been seen as masculine — hence the "man in the moon" motif common in Anglosphere cultures, the God Mani of the Nordic tradition, the God Suen of Harran, and so on.

In Platonism, everything below the moon's orbit is called the "sublunary realm," and the deities who preside over the moon in this context are usually Goddesses, but not always. Above the sublunary realm is the more "perfect" region of the cosmos — the realm of the wanderers (the planets) and fixed stars, beyond which are the realms that are not physical at all (although I'm not sure it is responsible to write "beyond" about the placeless). In 2022, we no longer profess a geocentric worldview, yet we can take what was once seen as a physical description of the universe as a *symbol* with a meaning similar to what Carl Sagan says when discussing the "pale blue dot" — only a slim sliver of atmosphere separates us from the void beyond, and every pleasure and pain within our lives happens on this world. Going "above" the sublunary in our rites and contemplative exercises thus means coming into wholeness through a symbolic ascent. The moon is our closest companion, responsible for tides and an assistant to animals from afar.

Achieving union with the One and ascending into the place beyond generation are goals within Platonism, but only a few (I'm thinking of Plotinus) are on the record as shying away from lunar ceremonies. Marinus, in the *Life of Proclus*, communicates how the divine successor of Plato (Proclus), on arriving at the Platonic school in Athens, honored the moon on seeing her in the sky with prostrations. This action convinced the school's leaders of Proclus' piety when they had previously not known what to make of the newcomer.

For the lunar cycle, the definitions I am about to use are slightly different from what you will see when you look at a wall calendar. In many calendars form the ancient world, including the one I have used for most of my activities, and in the modern-day Islamic calendar, the ritual month begins the day after the lightless moon when the crescent is visible. That first slim sliver is called the new moon. On your wall calendar, or with whichever moon phase extension you've added to Google Calendar or Outlook, the calendar will refer to the dark/lightless moon as the new moon, following modern astronomy's conventions. Twenty years ago, most Earth-based spirituality books I read in my teens also equated the dark and new moon, usually to refer to the lightless/dark moon. The dark moon, new moon, and full moon are the major times at which someone will worship lunar deities.

The dark moon is a perfect time to pray to one's ancestors. If you are living near where your family is buried, visiting their graves to offer flowers and clean up the headstones would be a lovely gesture. It is also a time to pray to apotropaic Goddesses. Hekate, for example, is both the Goddess who rules the baneful spirits of the material world and the salvation from them; Eris, who is most associated with the apple incident that started the Trojan War, is both a Goddess of discord as well as a Goddess who disrupts difficult situations so they can come to a useful resolution. You may also pray to underworld deities at this time. The dark moon, or in fact any time within the final few days of a lunar cycle, is a great time to clean one's home and donate those boxes you've been meaning to take care of.

The new moon is a time of beginnings. Its first sliver is a day to mark as a special occasion for your household Gods, the lunar deities, and any special Gods of affinity you may have. Dust the shrine, give an offering slightly fancier than usual, and cook something nice for yourself (and your family) or order some nice takeout. If you have a dessert, offer some to the Gods. Debrief, via freewriting, how last month went and what you can do in the month to come. Talk to the Gods about your plans and pray that you can take the lessons of last month forward in the best way possible.

Specific traditions may mark the new lunar month (either on the dark or new moon) with special rituals for specific Gods. If you seek out training and guidance in any of these traditions, expect that your lunar observances may change.

The full moon, depending on one's tradition, may or may not be emphasized. Many current and historical holidays for Gods will fall on the days leading up to or just after the full moon — but then again, there are often holidays at other times, too. As with the other two times of the month, consider how *you* want to honor the lunar rhythm.

If I have time, I give offerings to lunar deities, do a star/celestial grounding and centering practice, and drink water that has symbolically been imbued with moonlight. If I am pressed for time, I give an offering, pray, and chant for a few minutes. Someone I know (who is spiritual but not interested in praying to deities) once hosted monthly full moon circles with floor cushions, soft music, tea, and the recitation of creative works.

Moonrise and **moonset** are not often emphasized outside of niche ceremonial practices. Usually, you will need to know these times for determining when the moon is in the sky during your rituals. For example, I know that if I do a full moon ritual past 8:30 PM or so, it will not be visible through my east-facing window when I pray. I also know that, despite the beautiful ambiance of candles at night, that the new moon rises and sets with the sun. The Time and Date website[2] is the best tool to use for this. When I notice the moon in the sky, day or night, I often take a brief pause and say hi.

If a lunar or solar **eclipse** is visible in your area, it will happen on the full moon (the lunar eclipse) or the dark moon (the solar eclipse). The swallowing of the sun and darkening of the moon are natural effects of the dynamics of the Earth, Moon, and Sun. While I try to see eclipses when they're visible, I don't incorporate them into my rituals. Some religious traditions encourage fasting and purification during eclipses.

5.2.2 Venerating the Sun

Both the sun and moon have Gods and Goddesses, but masculine solar deities are more well-known to people — Gods like Helios, the Unconquerable Sun, Surya, or Ra. However, many cultures have had (or still do honor) a solar Goddess — Belesama, Sul, Sunna, Amaterasu, and others. In my estimation, whether a culture adopts a solar Goddess or God is correlated (with some exceptions) with latitude on Earth. The closer to the equator, or the more blisteringly dry an area's summers, the harsher the sunlight; the farther from it, the more marked

---

[2]https://www.timeanddate.com/moon/

its softer impact is on fertility and fecundity. If we think back to what was written in the section "An Important Caveat About Gods' Functional Roles," these distinctions likely evolved on the cultural level because the opening for that specific deity to express a relationship in solar terms was available locally.

We will focus on three types of veneration: the solstices and equinoxes, sunrise, and sunset. We already discussed eclipses when treating the moon.

The **solstices** only happen twice a year. If you are looking for a replacement for other joyous, complicated holidays, our planet's orbit has gifted us with two important days six months apart. The time of greatest darkness and the time of greatest light have different kinds of cultural associations. One of them welcomes in the season of winter, and the other welcomes summer. The beginning of winter is the start of a season of rest and incubation, prefacing the abundant outburst of spring. The beginning of summer starts off the heat and its calamities, but also prefaces the upcoming harvest season. Praying to the sun at dawn or sunset on these days — or having a complicated meal with your family — is also accessible to families with a variety of spiritual beliefs.

For the solstices, consider rotating out any wreaths, dried floral decor, reed diffuser sticks, and similar ambient items you have around the home. Going into the solstice with a clean, refreshed home is a beautiful thing. I dedicate a new laurel wreath to Apollon and hang it near my entryway on the winter solstice. Seasonal decorations can be taken out of storage and hung to celebrate. Many Americans are used to doing this in December, but less accustomed to it in June; it may take some time for you to acclimate to celebrating it.

The winter solstice is an excellent time to pray to a solar deity, Gods you are particularly fond of, and household Gods for good fortune in the season to come. If you can, keep a light-vigil (but be mindful of fire safety if you're using a flame) on the darkest night of the year and welcome the new sun as it rises, heralding the season of renewal. In many traditions, this is a time of gift-giving. Some people mark the return of light with special prayers that occur over a week, nine nights, or twelve nights.

On the summer solstice, pray to the solar deity, fond Gods, and household Gods. Summer-solstice prayers can be more apotropaic (meaning, averting ill fortune and calamity). The height of the sun's energy heralds the beginning, or increase, of stormy seasons, as there is a delay between when the sun is strongest and when we experience its environmental effects. You can also start a gift-giving tradition on the summer solstice if you like.

The **equinoxes** in the spring and autumn are dedicated to the renewal of life and harvest/dying season respectively. In the spring, you can pray to household and work-related deities for success on your new projects; in autumn, you give gratitude for what the world has brought, be it fruit or life lessons. Of course, there are some exceptions to the "death and the autumnal equinox" thing. Some cultures celebrate the dead during the dog days of summer or in the latter part of winter. For those of us in the United States, Halloween and All Soul's Day happen just over a month after the autumnal equinox.

Sunrise is most famous for being the time when Pythagore-ans greeted the Sun and did their prayers in antiquity. It is an auspicious time for prayer in other traditions, too. During fall and winter, sunrise happens at a time when I'm awake, so I take a few moments to pause and breathe with my eyes closed while facing it once I notice that it has cleared the building across the street, at least on days when the sky is clear. Even this brief pause makes me feel connected to the solar Gods. Sunrise is a good time for reciting chants, giving simple liba-tions, or contemplating a passage from a myth, philosophical text, or poem.

Sunset is trickier. For many of us, it happens during our commute. Evening prayers may be easier, especially as a final act before going to bed. This is a time that has traditionally been used for journaling and freewriting, so it's useful for contemplative activities and other restful devotional actions that prepare you for sleep.

5.3   Life Milestones

At least in the United States, the "milestones" by which we measure adulthood's seasons have changed dramatically over the past three generations. Rather than progressing from childhood to school to marriage to parenthood to retirement, the length of educational training and the prevailing circum-stances' impact on our lives mean that we might miss, or need to reinterpret, many life milestones that were once certain-ties.

Achieving a work or career milestone. Celebrate with an

offering to your professional God(s). Do something special that expresses gratitude for your success. You can also pray to the Gods when you finalize your job goals for the next year or quarter.

Bringing new family into your home. If you have given birth or have adopted a child, or if you have a young relative who needs you to be their guardian, taking a few moments to introduce them to the Gods at the household shrine can be a meaningful way of instilling a feeling of belonging. This can include a purificatory aspect, as per the last chapter, to invite good luck and ward off harm.

Bringing in a new pet. While I consider my cat to be my fur baby, pets are not the same as caring for a developing young human being. You can pray to the household Gods and to your patron deity or you can incorporate any deities who have historically had a role in animal husbandry.

Naming ceremonies. If you have named a child, or if someone in your family has taken a new name for any reason, a naming ceremony where Gods and ancestors are invited to give their blessings is a great way to formally mark the occasion. For name changes, it also provides closure.

Management of acute and chronic illnesses. Whether you are sick for a few weeks or have a long-term illness with flare-ups, marking the times when you get better with a special ritual can be a great "welcome back" event. I came down with the flu (the B strain that year was awful) in February 2020 and, after being in bed for 10 days, the first day I was able to light candles at my shrine and pray felt so meaningful. It didn't matter that I had to sit down to gather my strength halfway through. I was there, and I had made it.

Weddings and commitment ceremonies. Most people making commitments to a life partner do so in the context of marriage, but that is not the only option — many do commitment ceremonies instead because marriage comes with negative financial impacts in the form of welfare cliffs and poorly-designed benefits infrastructure, at least in the United States. Introducing your partner to the household Gods, sharing food with them, and purifying your living space can be incorporated into the ceremony, privately or as part of the larger ritual event.

Pregnancy and childbirth. You can pray for those who are pregnant or giving birth. If you are pregnant, you may consider altering your prayer ritual to incorporate offerings for the health and wellness of the future human you are growing in your lower abdomen. If you are actively trying to become pregnant or impregnate someone, incorporate fertility prayers and vent to the Gods about any hopes and fears.

Funerals. The purpose of a funeral is to give the body the rites that properly "send off" the deceased. They are an opportunity to show respect and care — and they should always be done according to the belief system that the person had in life, not what we wish it would have been. I grew up in a conservative area where it was not uncommon for funerals to include a spontaneous plea for religious conversion to the "correct" sect of the prevailing faith, or ones held by people who wanted to bring the deceased back into their faith after apostasy. The deceased was not placed at the center of the ritual. That is disrespectful. Likewise, when visiting burial plots, stick to making offerings of food, drinks, and flowers that the deceased may have enjoyed.

Death. Unlike funerals, honoring a death can be done alone. When one of my coworkers died unexpectedly in late 2021, I lit a candle for her the evening I heard and said a few words. As someone who cries easily, I was too afraid of not holding it together to say anything at her vigil, but privately, with a candle burning and my words directed at her, the tears were not as disruptive. I included her in the names of the deceased when I performed an annual ritual for the Chthonic Gods that February, about two months after her death. Anyone can be honored in this way.

Days of the week. In English, Monday, Tuesday, Wednesday, Thursday, Friday, Saturday, and Sunday are related to specific Gods.[3] In the Romance languages, the days of the week are also named after Gods. Honoring the God associated with the etymology is a great way to tune into the rhythms of the year.

Celestial clockwork. Stars rise, reach their highest point, and set. Planets do, too — and they appear to go through a specific lineup of constellations along the ecliptic, the Sun's apparent path. Some are fond of tracing the motions of a specific constellation.

It is important to approach prayer as a way of imbuing everything we do with what is sacred — of being active agents in our experience of spirituality and completing the chain that begins with the Gods and which emanates into matter. All things pray except the First, as Proclus wrote; we are all

---

[3]https://www.merriam-webster.com/words-at-play/saturday-special-word-history

praying in some capacity continuously, and continuous with our actions. What matters is becoming mindfully aware and using our rational faculties to steer our own ships under the guidance of the Gods.

5.4   The Mechanics of a Prayer

Our current discussion of ritual mechanics opens a floodgate of possibilities for what you can do along the wide gradient between *unstructured* and *highly-structured*. It provides opportunities for linking the daily practice you now have to the rhythms of your life and to the cycles of the year and lunar months.

If you feel overwhelmed, that is OK: The world is full of Gods, and every moment is teeming with deities, too. It is easy to get carried away.

In previous chapters, we focused more on getting you started with prayer than on the mechanics — in other words, we (mostly) focused on lightly-structured rituals and less formal prayer. In the chapter on purification, we started discussing something called *structured* ritual/prayer in the context of when you might want to take a break — structured prayers encompass most types of home shrine-based rituals, with varying degrees of complexity.

Prayer itself is a rhythmic practice through which we connect to the Gods. That active connection and engagement with them is both ordinary and transcendent. If we try to force an "end goal" instead of focusing on the rhythm of our actions and words for the God, we can quickly get in our own way and create stress and friction within the body, emotions, mind, and soul. Sometimes, people online or at community events wax excitedly about dreams filled with divine potency, guided meditations that lead to new and meaningful information, or Gods experienced, but their experiences are not the everyday. Life involves an awful lot of lines and waiting rooms. We can also let our expectations get out of hand.

An *unstructured* prayer is the kind of thing we do in passing (like at work or while in the airport), during times when the household shrine may be covered due to death or illness, and when an impromptu desire to pray strikes. It may or may not include offerings (if anything, a brief pour onto the ground from a to-go cup; a gift of a small treat beneath a tree while taking a hike; a whispered hymn). Here is how an unstructured prayer might play out:

1. **An invocation.** You greet the God by their name, adding any epithets or titles.

2. **Heartfelt words.** Speak from the heart what you want to say. This could include reading something if you have material with you (like a book on your phone).

3. **Sacred silence with the God.** Focus on your breathing for a few moments, and allow that to ground you into an open space. Focus on the God.

4. **An expression of gratitude.** Thank the God.

A *structured* prayer includes five basic elements:

1. **An invocation.** You greet the God by their name, adding any epithets or titles.

2. **An offering.** Offerings anchor the prayer in the world around us, opening space for connection to the God.

3. **Evoking what is holy.** Say some words, chant, read a hymn, or behold sacred images and stories about the God. I use the term *evoking* here because regardless of what you do — words, images, some combination — you are *bringing forth* an ambiance that welcomes the God.

4. **Sacred silence with the God.** Focus on your breathing for a few moments or minutes, and allow that to ground you into an open space. Focus on the God.

5. **An expression of gratitude.** Thank the God.

These elements are like the grammatical components of a sentence. Even with more structured prayers, a sentence may be simple or complex depending on the language. Within one language, sentences vary in length, and every language has unspoken elements that are meant for the hearer to infer. If I am pressed for time, for example, I may offer a very compressed prayer: I could say hello to Apollon, pour out some tea from a to-go cup, repeat a short chant three times, close my eyes and take a few breaths, and say thank you. That third step (here, the chanting) could even be compressed together with the fourth step (the silent pause).

When a sacred day comes up, a few minutes can be added onto your daily ritual if you judge you have time. I recommend placing it right after the invocation of the hearth Goddess and before you pray to any patron deities.

For more complex celebrations, we can build out from this prayer template to encompass other types of activities. For instance, if you are seeking blessings in spring for the herb garden that you are about to spend hours of care on, consider processing through your growing area after the offering or bringing your seedlings to the shrine to seek blessings. Perhaps you decide to honor the God at a meal for the summer solstice. You make sacred space at the park where you do your cookout, offer the God a portion of the meal, perform the remainder of the ritual, and eat in the God's presence when you're done. This is limited only by your imagination, common sense, and decency — always be respectful of the Gods in a ritual space, don't do anything wildly dangerous, and embrace the time you have to consciously focus on your connection to the sacred.

5.4.1 Praying for What Is Possible

The best time to start praying for something is at the beginning — weeks before you have that exam or performance evaluation, not at the last minute when you start to feel the pressure. There is a fable from Aesop called "The Shipwrecked Man and Athene" in which a shipwrecked sailor prays to Athene (his city's patron Goddess) to be saved from the ocean. Another man, swimming by, says, "Pray to the Goddess for success, but move your arms!" — the Gods can open up pathways for us, but we need to commit effort.

Prayers at the last moment may sometimes be answered, but there is nothing strange about needing to put in work to get what we want — as souls who inhabit material bodies and who are under the care of the Gods, it is in our nature to be able to *act in the material world* with these bodies. That is why we descend into generation and incarnate.

One way to make this part of your life is to say a short prayer to the Gods you already pray to whenever you're about to start planning a project or writing a complex, multi-part to-do list. It doesn't need to be fancy or structured, just a few words — and at the project's completion, thank the Gods you prayed to with an offering that is slightly fancier than what you usually do. It's up to you how to interpret *fancy*.

5.4.2 Praying for What Is Inevitable

Our sun, now a main sequence star, continues to eat her fuel, leaving just a little bit less to use an instant from now. Eventually, she will puff up as a red giant star and swallow many (or all) of her inner planets before her death as a nova billions of years from now. Earth may only be habitable for another billion years maximum — the sun's heat increases with its age, and Earth's core will one day no longer produce the magnetic field that protects Earth's surface from the impact of the solar wind. Any day now for the next 100,000 years, the star Betelgeuse in Orion could go supernova, and the explosion could be as bright as the half-moon, lasting for several months before fading.

Our incarnations a billion years from now will be on strange planets orbiting suns just blossoming into the caretakers of living beings. The universe is teeming with life.

When I was in my early twenties, I prayed to Hermes in his role as the God who conveys souls to the afterlife to ease my maternal grandfather's suffering as he passed. He had fallen, the doctor botched the anesthesia, and he was aspirating food into his lungs. He couldn't speak and clearly did not want any of us to see him in the state he was in. It was decided by the doctors, my mother, and my uncle that according to their father's wishes, given his prognosis, it was time to start palliative care. They removed the feeding tube. It could have taken him weeks to die; I imagined him starving to death and on medication to ease the pain. It sounded like torture. I prayed to Hermes for a swift death to ease my grandfather's suffering, and he was gone within two days.

At some point in our lives, we will all need palliative care. The sun will rise, for us and others, until it, too, dies. The world around us, the world of coming-to-be, is a place of impermanence and change. We will all have these difficult moments, and we all experience death.

5.5 Sample Ritual Outlines

Here are some sample rituals that I have done. They are personalized to Gods I worship and to my own situation. Others might call them slightly "eclectic" — I do not consider them to be that. Treat them the same way you would treat looking over someone else's personal essay on a topic. You may be drawn to similar themes, but it's preferable that your own practice will be based on *your* lived experience and relationship with the Gods.

Before my morning prayers, I do a brief purification. I light the hearth candle and pray to the hearth Goddesses. Then, I ritually purify water (which I change out about once a week, on Mondays) while praying to Hestia-Vesta, Eir, and Apollon, and continue on with the ritual. At other times of the day, I sprinkle myself with this prepared water if I decide to pray at my shrine again.

For offerings, I give an incense that seems appropriate to the context. For example, for lunar prayers, I choose a sweet-smelling blend that uses sandalwood. When praying to Apollon, I use frankincense or a blend that uses bay leaves. For Artemis and Dionysos, I choose something that evokes wild places. I give a libation of milk to the stars (yes, I am not above inserting humor about the Milky Way). Occasionally, I offer fruit juices or bubbly drinks; often, I offer the Gods water.

Note that the line breaks may lead one to believe this is poetry. While I did approach the ritual liturgy in a poetic style, it is usually not quite poetry. I find that adding line breaks helps for reading during ritual, at least until I've memorized something.

5.5.1 A Prayer to Creative, Intellectual, and Professional Gods

I clap twice and ring a bell twice. Then, I say, "I pray to you now, creative, intellectual, and professional Gods: Apollon, Mousai, Hermes, Mnemosyne, Athene, and Belesama. Please accept this offering of water, which flows back to you as you flow forth in abundance, and be well disposed."

I offer the water by placing it on the shrine. Then, I raise my hands in a prayer position to my forehead and say, "Οἰγνύσθω ψυχῆς βάθος ἄμβροτον· ὄμματα πάντα ἄρδην ἐκπετάννυμι ἄνω. Let the immortal depths of my soul be opened. May all of my eyes stretch completely upward on high."

Sometimes, if I am going through something, I'll say something unstructured about what's going on in my life. After a few breaths, I ring the bell twice, clap twice, and thank the Gods.

On the first and twelfth days of the lunar calendar, I offer incense and use prayer beads to chant οἰγνύσθω ψυχῆς βάθος ἄμβροτον· ὄμματα πάντα ἄρδην ἐκπετάννυμι ἄνω because those are the days I've reserved for more extended prayers to these Gods.

5.5.2 Evening Pause

I go to my shrine and say a prayer or two after sprinkling myself with the purification water. Then, I do a five-to-ten minute meditation, usually a mindfulness or lovingkindness one. I thank the Gods and go to bed. The prayers are usually for specific Gods — for example, the Muses — and I may also do prayer beads or say special prayers for Gods if I have decided to do a specific shorter-term devotional practice. This is also a good practice to do when one has purchased a new statue of or prayer beads to recite for a God.

5.5.3 New Moon

I integrate my new moon ritual into my morning ritual because I pray when the moon is in the sky. After I pray to the households Gods and all of the Gods, I make offerings to the lunar and liminal Gods, and I conclude the prayers with another offering at the end.

1. Welcoming the Gods, Lighting of the Flame

2. Prayer for Purification

3. Prayer to the Household Gods, Daimons, and Ancestors

4. Prayer to All of the Gods

5. Prayer to the Moon and Its Gods

6. Prayer to Apollon Noumenios[4]

7. Prayers to Gods of Affinity — Eir, Athene, Belesama, Apollon

8. Closing Prayer to the Lunar Gods and All of the Gods

I don't want to provide the exact text for my daily ritual practice, but I will show you the prayers made for the lunar Gods.

Prayer to the Moon

I pray to the luminous new moon,
beginning of new growth,
auspicious and divine,
male and female, feminine and masculine,
God of the soothing northern moon,
Goddess of the healing southern moon,
God of the east-rising moon,
Goddess of the west-setting moon.
May you, Gods of the Moon, accept this offering:
Mani, Sironā, Selene, whichever Gods are
enthroned, exalted, upon the Moon's holy body.

---

[4]I use a prayer from Labrys: http://www.labrys.gr/en/text_noume nia.html

May you, O Moon, and the Gods seated upon you
bless and protect us, guiding us to our Good,
and may Ianus and the Gods of transitions,
you who look forward and back,
bless and guide us in this new month.

Closing New Moon Prayer

I thank the Gods for witnessing this new moon ritual:
Goddesses of the hearth, first and last,
esteemed and gentle Mani,
God of the northern moon,
keeping day and night in solemn compassion;
beloved Sirona, adorned with stars,
Goddess of the night and the holy moon;
lush-braided Selene, luminous and enchanting,
Goddess who smiles down on the changeable world.
Apollon Noumenios, holy God of the new month,
accompanied by serpents, marking the boundary
between old and new, adorned with laurel,
and Ianus and the liminal Gods, looking forward.
Thank you to all of the Gods, spirits, and ancestors.
May you protect, guide, and bless my family and my girlfriend's family.
May you be our ever-present companions, O holy ones.
May you drive back sickness, evil, and despair,
may you bring us what is good and best,
and may the liminal Gods guided by Hermes
keep us safe from harm.

Merry meet, merry part, and merry meet again,
O Gods, spirits, and ancestors.

5.5.4   Full Moon: Aspirational

My full moon prayers are a separate evening ritual, and I pray
at around 8 or 8:30 PM after the moon has risen enough for
me to see it through my southeast-facing window.

When I do full moon rituals with my mother (admittedly
sporadically), who is Wiccan, we do something slightly different — in her initiatory tradition, sacred space is set up through
marking out a circle and visualizing a separation between the
ritual space and the exterior world in the form of a sphere.
Then, the elements are honored, and finally, the lunar deities
are honored. She is a devotee of Hekate, who is associated
with the moon and the sublunary world, so Hekate is a part
of that ritual.

Opening: Ground and Center

Imagine yourself growing branches into the Earth, and feel
the energy that you gather from her and the way your leaves
are tied to her seasons and cycles. Imagine the sky up ahead
— the sun, the vault of stars, the inky blackness, the planets,
the arms of our galaxy, the cosmic web — and imagine that
you are growing roots to nourish yourself on the blessings
from above. Feel the energy from the Earth and sky combine
within you, connecting you to the cosmos above and below.[5]

---

[5]While I have done groundings and centering practices since my pre-
teens, some imagery resonates with me more than others. I take a very
cosmology-oriented approach, as the way I conceptualize space includes a

Orphic Hymn to the Stars

I use the Athanassakis translation (Anonymous, n.d.), but the version translated by Thomas Taylor is freely available online — *Sacred Texts* and *Theoi.com* are two common resources for public domain items.

Prayer to the Moon

I pray to the luminous full moon,
swelling with abundance,
auspicious and divine,
male and female, feminine and masculine,
God of the soothing northern moon,
Goddess of the healing southern moon,
God of the east-rising moon,
Goddess of the west-setting moon.
I pray to you, luminous Moon, seat of many Gods,
Mani, Sironā, Selene, and many others call you theirs.
At the fullness of your beauty, shining upon all,
reflecting the luminous sun, sublunary ruler,
give my soul sustenance from your holy light.
Do not let me become entranced by illusion,
but guide me to the luminousness of Intellect
seated beyond the spheres, beyond the subjective,
vehicled in noetic and noeric fire, resplendent.

---

decent repertoire of astronomy and cosmology images about the cosmic web, galaxy clustering, and the dynamics of how the Sun orbits the center of the Milky Way. One approach that I love, and which I now draw on for when I do groundings and centerings, is *Stellar Magic: A Practical Guide to the Rites of the Moon, Planets, Stars and Constellations* by Payam Nabarz (Nabarz, 2009).

May you, O Moon, accept this offering.
May you, O Moon, and the Gods seated upon you
bless and protect those of us in embodiment,
guiding us to our Good, guiding us home.

Lunar Envesselment

Ideally, I hold the bowl of water in a way that puts it line-of-sight with the moon outside. If this is not possible, I close my eyes and envision moonlight filling the bowl. I chant *Aiglê, Pasiphae, Eileithyia, Selene, Mani, Ueronadā, Sironā, Luna* in a musical way, pour out some of the water for the lunar Gods and the stars, and drink the rest while envisioning the power of the celestial vault and the moon filling me.

I follow this with Chandra Bhedana, a closure of the right nostril for 20 inhalations while thinking of clear white light coming in and out, purifying. Afterward, I come into stillness and envision being connected to the whole of generation that is humming with the Gods while firmly situated and anchored in my own center. This meditation can last as long as one likes.

Gratitude Prayer

I thank the Gods for witnessing this full moon ritual:
Goddesses of the hearth, first and last,
the stars who circle in the night sky above,
boundless and bounded, far and yet so near,
to Selene of lush braids,
she who waxes and wanes,

who counts out the month in her dance
around our Earth as the sunlight shimmers upon her surface;
to esteemed and gentle Mani,
God of the northern moon,
keeping day and night in solemn compassion;
to beloved Sironā, adorned with stars,
Goddess of the night and the holy moon.

Closing Prayer

Thank you, O Gods.
May you protect my family and my girlfriend's family.
May you be our ever-present companions, O holy ones.
May you drive back sickness, evil, and despair,
and may you bring us what is good and best.
The ritual is concluded.

5.5.5   Full Moon: When It's Been a Long Day

I have a backup ritual for full moon observances when life
is hectic. I open the ritual with a brief prayer to the hearth
Goddesses, a purification, and a few grounding breaths.

Opening

I ground and center and do a brief hearth lighting. This section is very compact.

Prayer to the Moon

I pray to the luminous full moon,
swelling with abundance,

auspicious and divine,
male and female, feminine and masculine,
God of the soothing northern moon,
Goddess of the healing southern moon,
God of the east-rising moon,
Goddess of the west-setting moon.

I pray to you, luminous Moon, seat of many Gods,
Mani, Sironā, Selene, and many others call you theirs.
At the fullness of your beauty, shining upon all,
reflecting the luminous sun, sublunary ruler,
give my soul sustenance from your holy light.
Do not let me become entranced by illusion,
but guide me to the luminousness of Intellect
seated beyond the spheres, beyond the subjective,
vehicled in noetic and noeric fire, resplendent.
May you, O Moon, accept this offering.
May you, O Moon, and the Gods seated upon you
bless and protect those of us in embodiment,
guiding us to our Good, guiding us home.

Chant

I go to the window if the Moon is visible and chant the verses
from Mike Oldfield's *Incantations* Part One, but may vary the
deity names according to the melody. It's very meaningful
because my mom played this album frequently when I was a
young child, and she would also sometimes sing this chant
to the moon, either spontaneously or during ritual. (She still
does!) Sometimes, I do this part before the actual ritual be-

cause I see the moon rise from my apartment window, which always takes my breath away.

Gratitude Prayer

I thank the Gods for witnessing this full moon ritual:
Goddesses of the hearth, first and last,
the stars who circle in the night sky above,
boundless and bounded, far and yet so near,
to Selene of lush braids,
she who waxes and wanes,
who counts out the month in her dance
around our Earth as the sunlight shimmers upon her surface;
to esteemed and gentle Mani,
God of the northern moon,
keeping day and night in solemn compassion;
to beloved Sironā, adorned with stars,
Goddess of the night and the holy moon.

Closing Prayer

Thank you, O Gods.
May you protect my family and my girlfriend's family.
May you be our ever-present companions, O holy ones.
May you drive back sickness, evil, and despair,
and may you bring us what is good and best.
The ritual is concluded.

5.5.6   Ancestor Ritual

This book has not discussed ancestor veneration — only in passing — but it can be a fulfilling practice. Many people start this veneration practice when they begin praying to many Gods, and others don't until a death happens and they want some way to feel close to family. There are many authors who provide robust frameworks for ancestor-related practices. One reason I think ancestor veneration is increasing so much in the United States is that it's far easier to pray at a designated area in one's home than to travel to a grave. Many of us are disconnected from the places where our ancestors lived because we had to move for work or education, and this is one way to make remembrance special without needing to buy plane tickets or drive halfway across the country. As is hopefully obvious from the way I offer prayers, "ancestor" has a very loose meaning — it doesn't have to be someone related to you. I recommend looking at guidance online if you have a difficult family history — there are many perspectives on how to manage those issues, and you can still have a fulfilling and connection-driven ancestor worship practice.

When I pray to the ancestors, I give an offering of Nippon Kodo Cafe Time incense (five-minute cones) or something similar and sake, water, milk, or mead, and I do this offering during the final days of the lunar cycle before the new moon. After the prayers, I may give the ancestors life updates. It ideally happens at night, but I sometimes do it in the morning. The day before the dark moon, I do not pray at my main shrine. I only pray to ancestors and underworld Gods.

The prayers below are slightly different from the ones I

actually offer, but ancestor prayers feel more private. This is enough to provide a decent idea.

For Ancestors Related to Me

I make this offering to
my grandparents of my paternal line,
my maternal line, my great-grandparents
each twist and turn of marriage,
the many lives branching out and upward
into the past in root-thickets of consciousness,
making a spirit and vessel of those who have chosen
to be incarnated in my family.
I pray to my recent ancestors whose faces I know,
to my distant ancestors whose faces and names have receded.
I pray to the ancestors who kept the old rites for the Gods,
for the ones who had lost them unknowing.
Please accept this offering of mead and incense.
Come, ever-gentle, and grant blessings to us, your descendants.
Assist us along the paths that we must take
in this guest-house we call a lineage.
Each of us, like sparrows, has entered this hall only to fly out again.
Incarnating here among the many choices of life,
we have given and will give what we have.
I honor your memory and seek your favor.

Prayer to the Disir

I pray to the holy Disir,
protectors of your descendants,
Goddesses, spirits, and esteemed female dead,
I come to you in gratitude.
Thank you for your guidance and protection.
May you protect the women of my family.
May you bless the women of my family.
May you instruct the women of my family.
May you be present to us in our daily lives.
We welcome you, trusted divinities.
We welcome you, our great elders.

Prayer to Ancestors of Intellect

For my intellectual lineage,
bright minds who illumine the soul,
who train it ever upward —
I make this offering to you, O illustrious ones,
pure souls shining in the words I read.
Please accept this prayer of gratitude.
You guide me through the pages.
You walk me along the upward path
even though the brambles sting and my mind tires,
so I may know the gifts of true beauty
hidden in passages strung like ivy and laurel,
uncovered by those known and unknown to me,
men and women of steady minds,
of hearts so filled with the love of the Gods

and the spaciousness beyond being that is no space,
intellectuals, philosophers, true theologians,
poets and creators of the most beautiful agalmata
holding the keys to the Gods who rule all things.

Closing

Thank you, ancestors, for your blessings. Accept this offering,
O predecessors.

5.6   Exercise: Do a Special Ritual

At the beginning of this chapter, I encouraged you to jot down
some notes with ideas you have about honoring the sacred.
Choose *one* thing coming up after your next payday (or grocery
shopping haul). Is it the full or new moon? Are you starting or
ending a project? Have you just adopted a cat? Is it the start
of exam period?

Using the information here and your budding experience
with prayer, create a ritual outline. After consulting your budget, add anything you need for that ritual to your grocery/sup-
plies list. Hold time on your calendar and do what you need
to do.

Why wait until your next pay period? Many of us base our
activities around our pay cycles. If you have room in your
current cycle's budget for something special, it's fine to adjust.
I get paid monthly and set aside a certain amount of money
for incidental expenses. Usually, by the time the fourth week
of the month rolls around, between coworkers fundraising
for their children's creative enrichment programs, impulse

book purchases, and realizing all of my socks (somehow) once again have holes in them, I'm at the point where I am thinking carefully to avoid going overbudget — and I'm sure many people experience similar ebbs and flows. While offerings are factored into my monthly spending and I plan ahead for higher-cost holidays like the solstices, they are probably not budget categories for you yet. In any case, over the next few months, track what you spend on offerings and other spiritual wellness items, and the average of that is what you should put down as your habitual spending.

If you don't have a pay period, remember to do what you can with what you have. Flowers gathered in a natural area, nicely-steeped tea, or a small portion of what you have on hand can all make lovely offerings. Focus instead on the spirit of these words from Simplicius:

> [I]t is not possible to perform [the sacred rites] "beyond one's means" on a frequent basis. Those who are excessively competitive with respect to divinity seem at one and the same time to convict it of accepting bribes and to be unaware of providing these things for the honour of the divinity: they are meant to be the first fruits, i.e., merely a sampling, of the things given to us by [the] God. (Simplicius, 2014: 95, 11–16)

and

> [The God] often receives gifts from the pious, not because [the God] needs them (the gifts, that is), but rather because the people offering them are

stretching up to reach [the God] in this way through external things, too, just as they do in their souls (Simplicius, 2014: 107, 2–9).

Cultivating a proper symbolic register can be important, but what is most important is treating offerings as tools to reach the Gods. Expensive offerings mean nothing without piety. The proper attitude is one of gratitude, lovingkindness, and trust.

Chapter 6

Lifelong Learning

Throughout the first part of this book, we built up the foundations of ritual practice. In many chapters, I provided thought prompts and mentioned opportunities for follow-up research, but we didn't dwell on them then — we focused on establishing a solid daily practice.

Ritual practices, like all routines, will iterate. You will go through seasons of your life when five minutes *is* all you have and other seasons when you can, and want, to do more. There will be days when showing up at shrine will be the last thing on your mind — maybe you're anxious over an unexpected bill, you've lost a job, or someone in your family is going through a hard time — and other times when you feel the abundant presence of the universe all around you.

In music, it often happens that the composer or improvisational performer will select specific melodies to linger over — something to weave in and out as the music continues, a melodic thread that you can rely on for the unity of the piece. Think of lifelong learning like that: we don't have the time or ability to follow up on everything, so we select what makes sense for us to explore.

For some people, these emphases may include engaging with learning material and/or joining formal or informal groups. Learning happens in all of these places, and as social animals, we all need some combination of this — but for now, we will focus on personal learning and how to develop a learning trajectory.

> ### What If You're Satisfied Already?
>
> If you are completely good with your five minutes, the suggestions in this chapter can be adapted to any kind of adult learning — whether you are deepening your knowledge of the Python programming language or trying out mathematical crochet.

Many reading this book may already be thinking of ways to supplement their core prayer practice. This is the first part of three covering what to do now that you have set down some foundations. After this, we will talk about virtue and groups.

Practicing daily rituals and cultivating a conscious connection to the Gods is slightly different from studying something like religion, theology, or philosophy. These oceans are vast, and it is important to have a map. This chapter focuses on crafting that trajectory.

Let's start by thinking about what we want to study.

In your notes on this book, and in your practice thus far, you may have jotted down questions, or the same thoughts may be cycling through your head over and over. Here are some examples:

- Why is Kaye talking about Platonism? Didn't Plato just write political philosophy? How does this match what I learned in school?

- While praying to Ptah, I came across hymns that used terms unknown to me. What do these mean in Egyptian traditional religion, and how can I build up my knowledge so I understand what I'm reading?

- Stoicism talks about Zeus a lot. Is there a theistic way to approach Stoicism that is different from Silicon Valley self-help?

- Kaye mentioned a quotation from Proclus about seasons. What are my options for seasonal prayers to specific Gods?

- This book has been very heavy on the Hellenic Gods due to Kaye's background. How do these concepts translate to the Gods *I* want to worship? If some concepts are less appropriate, why? What could I investigate instead?

- That's a good point about needing to consider honoring Gods associated with yoga. What are some next steps that I need to take for my practice so I am doing responsible and ethical cultural reception?

Creating a learning plan is an important skill that is rarely ever taught. Before I got really into a Platonizing practice, I had heard from someone that everything I needed to know about the Hellenic Gods is contained within Plato. The first dialogue I read after hearing that, Plato's *Symposium*, was astonishingly different from the scant excerpts assigned in school — it was *fun* — and I wanted to read more. I was so angry about having been deceived by inadequate educational exposure to Plato! Still, without a committed study habit and with a lot changing in my twenties as I finished school and started working, it was hard to read *anything* for fun, let alone Plato. The hours I spent on social media didn't help. It wasn't until my late twenties when I left Facebook that I started to rediscover my focus and mental energy.

6.1 Content Is Written By People

Generally speaking, there are two types of content you will encounter when you are trying to learn more: academic content and practitioner content. Some academics also worship many Gods (and sometimes the Gods they study), but due to pressures in academia, it can be hard to figure out who they are unless you start talking to people. Be mindful of the tone used in academic publications — are the authors being respectful? Are they punching down on their research topic? This can provide a clue.

Academic content is most frequently released in the form of journal articles, books (jargon term: *scholarly monographs*), or gray literature (think PowerPoint slides, reports, and conference talk notes — often on faculty websites, Academia.edu, or preprint archives). Practitioner content may be in the form of social media posts, blog pieces and short manuals, and published books. Both academics and practitioners will post lectures to YouTube and other platforms of varying degrees of accuracy.

It's important to be open to diverse perspectives and to not dismiss people because of their specific views. Use critical thinking when you engage with someone's content. In order to make informed decisions about where to direct your attention, it can be helpful to do some research on authors and organizations. This might include looking up the author or organization's name online, reading their free material, and examining criticism of their work. There are some lists online that claim they can reduce this work or that offer specific lists of "red-flag" terms, but don't rely on these — many people, including myself, are sometimes clueless about word usage subtext and lexical drift. We live in a very politically-charged, polarized atmosphere, and online interactions can make these divisions seem sharper. Getting hyper-anxious about organizations, authors, and bloggers is not productive or useful when you are doing research on the range of practitioner perspectives about a Goddess or digging into protocols for cleansing a new home. I read plenty of people with whom I disagree on a variety of issues because some of their perspectives on praxis are pious and valuable, even if I sometimes find the person irritating or challenging.

However, there are some specific problems in the present century. Content on Nordic Gods, for example, is divided between far-right white supremacist groups on the one hand and very progressive material on the other. Proceeds from purchasing extreme right-wing materials put money into the pockets of people who are harming nonwhite American citizens (among others). The extremely progressive material

⌐ine that you are only one awakening away from be-
⌐ning a Marxist-anarchist, but it's a more ethically sound
purchase choice. Most moderates in American society accept
the realities of cultural, ethnic, and racial diversity. In Norse
polytheism, those who are not in the far right are encouraged
by their communities to swing farther left because it's seen
as important for amplifying the message that extremism isn't
welcome in the religion.

Another challenge is the tendency for individuals to be
pressured to monetize content in order to get by and make
rent, especially with today's wealth inequalities — often before
a person has enough mastery of the material to be ready to
provide a spiritual service to others. The Internet is filled with
people who got into something 10 months ago and are trying
to make money off of it. We always need to put the spiritual
wellness and integrity of the ones we are teaching *first* in any
learning environment, as being in an teacher/student relationship means that the recipient of a teaching has invested care
of their soul's development in *us*. It's not to be taken lightly or
carelessly.

Experience itself is multifaceted — someone may have a
PhD in a topic related to the Gods or initiatory training in a
specific tradition, and another person may have spent 20-30
years experimentally working through a non-initiatory practice on their own (although, truth be told, nothing happens in
a vacuum). In library science, we call this "authority is con-
structed and contextual" (an information literacy frame as put
out by American College and Research Libraries, also known
as ACRL) (ACRL, 2015). It's on us to discern which experts we

want to trust, regardless of how that person acquired their expertise.

If you are engaging with informal content (like a blog), be sure to check the person's About page and their blog's first few posts. Usually, bloggers will write an origin story at some point to talk about where they are starting from, and even if that origin story is a decade old on their Wordpress (meaning you don't know how it compares to who the person is now without reading their bio for their more recent activities), it gives you valuable information about them. For example, I used to call myself a "Hellenic polytheist" and write from a lens that I no longer agree with. I've changed how I present myself significantly over the past few years due to an increased awareness of and desire to respect modern Hellenes/Greeks. I have zero expertise in how a Greek person mediates their Hellenic identity, whichever God or Gods they worship, or what worshipping Gods means to them as individuals or as a community, and I now endeavor to make it clear where I am coming from. I am building up what a theistic cultural reception of the Hellenic Gods can look like in America (hopefully in a tactful way), so that's where I focus my attention. That's in my bio. The first post on my blog is something I wrote in my mid-to-late 20s about my values and practice, which looked very different at the time.

6.2   Using the Library

Libraries can be accessed at the local, state, and national levels. You may also have access to the library of the institution where you work or study, or you may have a private library membership. Your state library will license resources for the entire state to use remotely — it's worth knowing what those resources are. The same goes for your local library. All of this can be found on the library website.

When you visit your library's website, check their policies on interlibrary loan and item delivery between libraries in the same state system. Interlibrary loan is often no-fee at academic institutions, but some local and state libraries will apply a fee to using it to offset the costs. Similarly, item delivery between locations may either be free or have a nominal fee.

Library databases contain a variety of content. Some databases blend newspaper, magazine, and scholarly materials together; others separate them. Scholarly resources are often *peer-reviewed*, which means that the paper someone submitted to the journal was read and scrutinized by other experts to ensure it was on the right track. This is why it can take some time for new research to appear — papers can be kept in peer review for months or years. Dissertations, while not peer-reviewed, are evaluated before a PhD candidate is allowed to graduate. They usually describe very innovative research and are wonderful to read, especially for research topics that are less well-discussed. They have very extensive bibliographies.

As a librarian, I can give you a few tips for using online databases, regardless of which ones you have access to:

- Find the documentation (or help files) for the database and read the sections in it on advanced searching.

- While many databases are moving to a single search box

to remind users of Google, databases are still structured information resources that allow you to query specific fields. On either the database main page or in the advanced search, take a look at your options in the drop-down menus beside the search box. You may be able to limit by publication title, author, region, and other facets. I like searching in ProQuest or Ebsco databases for everything *except* the full text unless I'm searching for information on an obscure Goddess. In those cases, I want any anecdotal reference I can find anywhere in the full text.

- When interacting with search results, do not forget the filters on the left-hand side! Try to filter to scholarly/peer-reviewed resources, magazines, and so on — just to see how the resources you are finding differ.

- Use a reference management tool like Zotero to organize the resources you find and prevent yourself from having to log in to repeat searches and find information again. Zotero has a built-in PDF annotation tool, and it supports note-taking.

- Pay attention to the keywords that the databases assign to items that you find useful. These are jargon terms that may be submitted by the publisher/author, or they could be subject classifications assigned by the database provider. Regardless, they can help you standardize your vocabulary and "think like a machine" to identify other relevant works.

- Click on any text that is hyperlinked in the item records

to see what happens. Authors, keywords, you name it!
This is how digital serendipity works.

Keywords, Library of Congress subject terms, and other helpful information are also available in the main library catalog.
Whenever you find a book that is helpful to you, look in your
local library catalog or on WorldCat for the item. Jot down
notes of what terms are applied to the book and use those
search terms next time you are looking things up.

Google Scholar behaves similarly to a library database, but
it is a search engine, and it uses automated scraping with no
human quality control. This means that Google Scholar contains a lot of information, but it can misidentify some items
as scholarly when they are not, and it sometimes grabs the
wrong information about an article. Still, if you are outside of
academia, it lets you know what scholars are producing. The
documentation on how to use advanced searching is essential
for getting what you need.

As an example search, if you wanted to search for Belesama with both name spelling variants, but wanted to exclude
mentions of Britain, this is the advanced Google (or Google
Scholar) search you would do:

```
(Belesama OR Belisama) AND Goddess -Britain
```

The same search would work in a scholarly database, but the
word *NOT* may be used instead of the minus sign to exclude
terms. Some of my examples will use multiple words in quotation marks to mark a phrase, but you can also use quotation
marks around a single word to keep Google from *stemming* the
word, or searching for variants. I sometimes use quotation

marks around the word "Gods" so Google is forced to find the plural. Databases, on the other hand, frequently make you explicitly mark that you want stemming to occur by using an asterisk or question mark — *God**, for example, will match *God, Goddess, Gods, Goddesses, Godfrey,* and so on. *Wom?n* will match *woman, women, womxn,* and other variants. There may be some variation, though — check the help files.

If I wanted to do a slightly more complicated search, this time for Apollon's worship[1] in Asia Minor:

```
(Apollo OR Apollon) AND (cult OR cultus OR worship)
AND "Asia Minor"
```

If you don't have access to an article directly, this is when you use interlibrary loan, check the author's website for a repository version of the article (more and more common due to the increase in open access), or ask the author directly. Books are easiest to find via interlibrary loan or a library purchase request, and especially for small publishers, going through official channels to acquire the book makes a huge difference to the publishing house and authors.

6.2.1   Do You Have Alum JSTOR Access?

At least in the United States, many people who have graduated from college have graduated from institutions that provide alum access to JSTOR. Look at your alum website, and if you can't find anything about that, contact the library. This will

---

[1]The term *cultus* or *cult,* when used to refer to ancient cultures' ritual and devotional practices, is a neutral, frequently-used term.

broaden what you can do on your own without interlibrary loan.

6.3 Finding Book Reviews

If you Google an author's name or a book title with the phrase "book review" (with the quotes around "book review"), you will find reviews that Google has indexed beyond just what's on Amazon. If you don't have ideas for a specific book, just put in a topic (such as divination, worshipping Kemetic Gods, Shiva in yoga, prayers for Gods):

```
"book review" AND Kemetism AND beginners


"book review" AND (Kemetism OR "Egyptian Polytheism"
AND beginners


"review" AND polytheism AND theology site:goodreads.com


"book review" AND beginners AND ("Norse paganism"
OR "Norse polytheism") -site:amazon.com
```

Many of the books in the Google results will be worth reading, although it's good to know an author's perspective before you jump into their work.

6.4 My Plan for Plato

This is the advice that, after several years studying Platonism-related topics, I would give to someone embarking on an in-depth study. What I hope you take away from the example is how important flexibility is, yes, but I also want to convey that we don't all have it completely figured out immediately. It's okay to do something when you're not totally sure where it's going.

If one has heard that Platonists were spiritual sages in antiquity — say, from Linda Johnsen's *Lost Masters: Sages of Ancient Greece*, one may attempt to dive directly into Plotinus like I did when I was in my early 20s and have a disorienting and discouraging experience. No matter how exciting an author seems, starting with the fundamentals is crucial to understanding what is going on at all. I had only read the *Symposium, Ion,* and a few other Platonic dialogues at that point. While I had read Sallust's *On the Gods and the World,* it hadn't been framed to me at the age of 20 as a Platonic text, so I thought it was simply amazing polytheistic theology without knowing where it came from.

The made me realize that I needed to have read more Plato. So. I bought one of those giant books with every work by Plato and started reading.

That was also a mistake.

The breakthrough happened when I learned that there was such a thing as a dialogue reading order (Rowe, 2015). There is a modern, which-one-did-he-write-when order (which I don't recommend), and there are several systematic treatments that were used in the ancient world when reading Plato — one with a lot of dialogues and another with a selection. The selection of dialogues is the Iamblichean reading order, named for Iamblichus, a Syrian Platonist who was instrumental for reinvigorating traditional religious practice through the careful application of Platonic doctrine. He assigned twelve dialogues: *Alcibiades I, Gorgias, Phaedo, Cratylus, Theaetetus, Sophist, Statesman, Phaedrus, Symposium, Philebus, Timaeus,* and *Parmenides*.

At first, I read the dialogues on their own, and I reached the *Symposium* with that method. I picked up one of the Platonic commentaries (the one by Hermias on Syrianus' *Phaedrus* lectures) by happenstance and discovered that its exegesis of the material was extremely useful and groundbreaking. However, when I read the *Parmenides* commentary, I felt like the rug had been pulled out from under me because my understanding of the rungs on the ladder from the One to Matter was almost nonexistent in any meaningful way. I continued reading Platonic texts and found some helpful modern scholars' work at good price points that helped me understand the metaphysics a bit more. Then, I started listening to the *Secret History of Western Esotericism* podcast (despite not identifying as an esotericist) because its episodes on Plato were very helpful. A few people on social media were extremely helpful and generous with their time in explaining some concepts when I had questions. I read the *Parmenides* before the *Timaeus* and only read the *Timaeus* after the *Republic* and *Laws*, which I added due to never having read them. At about that time, I realized that there was no one correct reading order for the commentaries and that swallowing them down as simultaneously as possible would give me the best rough outline. The pandemic happened all of a sudden (when I was reading the *Laws* and finishing up reading some of Proclus' essays on the *Republic*, which had been translated into French); spiritual Platonists started posting content to YouTube — Tim Addey, Mindy Mandell — and I found other content from Pierre Grimes. The combination of reading, audio, and visual content was extremely helpful, as was the lockdown isolation. I learn very fast when in immersion environments, which I figured out in college, and because I have a prayer practice, I was able to cross-reference the mystical parts of Platonism against my own experiences. I eventually found some virtual groups to engage with, all based on Zoom. I continued — and continue — swallowing down commentaries and other Platonic writings.

6.4.1 My Advice on Reading Platonic Texts for Others

What I would encourage, based on my experience, is to read *Alcibiades I*, *Gorgias*, and the *Phaedo*. Then, stop reading those and pick up Radek Chlup's *Proclus: An Introduction*, which introduces key elements of the system in a manageable way. Take note of the tables included in that book — they are very useful. Read the *Anonymous Prolegomena to Platonic Philosophy*, an ancient text that introduces how Plato is read in the Platonic curriculum. Several articles by Danielle Layne (Danielle A Layne, 2014; Danielle A. Layne, 2017) contain useful tables for understanding how Platonists read dialogues, and Edward Butler wrote an article for a general audience on the polycentricity of the Gods (Butler, 2016) that can be used to drive those concepts home. Deviate from this to read Iamblichus' *On the Mysteries/De Mysteriis*, which will help to ground all of the cerebral in practical prayer and attentiveness to the Gods. Ensuring that one maintains an active prayer practice while learning is absolutely crucial to gaining insights.

Read the *Alcibiades I* again, this time in conjunction with one of the commentaries (remember: interlibrary loan) — Proclus and Olympiodorus both wrote on it. Read Tim Addey's *The Unfolding Wings*, Sallust's *On the Gods and the World*, and Mindy Mandell's *Discovering the Beauty of Wisdom*. For podcasts, listen to the *Secret History of Western Esotericism* from the beginning, *The History of Philosophy Without Any Gaps*' early episodes, and look up any podcast interviews with Gregory Shaw or Edward Butler. From there, read the *Gorgias* and its commentary, the *Phaedo* and its commentaries, and continue in that fashion for the dialogues that Iamblichus recommended until you finish the *Philebus*. For the Parmenides, first read Aristotle's *Metaphysics* and Syrianus' response to it (two volumes, one on *Metaphysics 3-4* and another on *Metaphysics 13-14*), then read the *Parmenides* alongside Proclus' commentary. While reading the commentaries, cycle to treatises from Plotinus as they are mentioned in footnotes and endnotes. Read the *Republic* and *Laws*. Read the *Timaeus* and its commentary. The *Elements of Theology* and *Platonic Theology* are useful to approach now, as are any other texts by Aristotle you may be interested in (or not). Read Plotinus' *Enneads* and any of Proclus' essays or Damascius' other works. It's all an iterative process, and once one has the trunk fairly solid, the branches may grow where they take you closer to the light.

If you're only curious about the philosophical system and do not want the deep details, reading something like *Discovering the Beauty of Wisdom* alongside the *Alcibiades I*, *Phaedo*, *Apology*, and *Phaedrus* will get you a decent idea. I recommend that anyone read Iamblichus' *On the Mysteries*, though, and the *Anonymous Prolegomena to Platonic Philosophy* is a very good read. To be perfectly frank, whenever I got discouraged writing this primer on worshipping Gods because it seemed daunting or I doubted my relevance, skill, or capacity, I just thought back to Iamblichus to anchor and guide me. Almost everything we need to know about honoring the Gods is in Iamblichus or Proclus.

6.5   Creating Your Plan

The above may have been overwhelming. For one, Platonism involves reading a lot of scholarly monographs (which I didn't really even discuss) — someone studying Norse concepts of the soul or divination or modern devotional poetry will skew their reading more towards practitioners' publications. If you are studying Stoicism, the modern popularization has made it very easy to find writings about Stoic philosophy, but there is less available on the open web about its spiritual aspects.

Here is what I hope you took away from the prior section on getting more familiar with Platonism:

- Choose multiple formats. Audio, video, and writing are all represented above.

- While starting out with a survey book of a topic may be ideal, you do actually need a sense of the material itself. In the example above, my advice to read a few dialogues before getting into other types of content is based on that premise.

- You don't need to have it figured out all at once. You can use the works cited by someone to build out and adjust your reading list.

- Learning can be overwhelming, as it pushes us outside of our comfort zones. That's why it's learning. During the lowest points, do what you can to ease the discomfort and remember why you're doing this.

- Put your audiobook and ebook apps on your phone's home screen and hide everything that isn't reading material. Ensure that books you need to read are located within arm's reach on the couch.

Above all, keep your plan sensible. If you have half an hour a day to study between when you put your kids to bed and when you want to spend time with your spouse — or if you know that your only alone time at home will be when you wash the dishes with headphones in — do not choose a plan that is unrealistic about the formats you need or the reading speed you have.

If you have a condition that impacts your focus or stamina, put your health first and seek out advice from others with similar conditions about how they build time for learning and personal enrichment into their lives. For example, magazines like *ADDitude* (for people with ADHD) or *Momentum Magazine* (for people with multiple sclerosis) are good choices for getting the support you need, as they synthesize information from medical experts and community members. Typically, you can find such publications via Google or in resources lists on nonprofit websites.

If you frequently use social media, it's likely that your attention span will have deteriorated from when you were younger. Consider doing a social media fast for a few days while you start up your new study habit. If you frequently binge-watch shows, reducing your screen time to 1-2 episodes per day can improve you experience of the show and give you some much-needed reading time, as research shows binge-watching can reduce the amount of enjoyment we get out of savoring new episodes.

Here are some guidelines for getting the most out of your learning plan:

- While you read, take notes. Keep a notebook or write in the margins so you can roll around in the text and react to what you're reading. If you are using ebooks, export the notes when you are done so you can review them.

- Never underestimate exercise. I've found that doing some exercise in the early evening helps me bounce back from mental fatigue — something as simple as a walk or a few sun salutations.

- Build on what you're learning. Start writing essays about things that interest you. You're not being graded. *Not being graded is magical.*

- Celebrate small wins. When you have finished something tricky, do something nice for yourself — put on your favorite song, dance, give yourself a hug, or say something good about yourself in the mirror.

While you are studying, you will likely come across courses (free and paid), reading groups, and other ways to learn from experts. Take advantage of the opportunities that are affordable to you, and don't assume that a higher cost equals a better learning experience. Be wary about becoming a "groupie" for a specific expert — direct your devotion at the Gods, not at human beings, and always be aware that the ones you are learning from are humans with merits and flaws. If someone is trying to induce the fear of missing out (FOMO) in their marketing materials, or if they're positioning themselves as the only safe harbor, be suspicious. They probably don't have the exclusive knowledge they're claiming to possess.

6.6   Exercise: Create A Content List

Brainstorm a topic that you want to know more about, ideally related to worshipping Gods. Identify content items that you can engage with to learn more about it. They could be books, videos, podcasts, courses — you name it. Look up reviews for the books and learn more about the podcast, video, and book creators. Narrow the resources down to five.

Then, find learning time in your schedule — one or two blocks of time per week. Use that time to engage with the materials you have selected.

Chapter 7

Virtue

> Virtue might be described as the perfection of the
> soul and proper balance of its life and as the high-
> est and purest activity of reason and intellect and
> discursive intelligence. Let the acts of virtue be
> taken, above all, as being boniform, excellently
> fine, intellectual, noble, full of moderation, par-
> ticipant in appropriateness, promoting moral ad-
> vancement, aiming at the best end, and graceful
> (Iamblichus, 2009:Letter 16).

Cultivating virtue and adhering to an ethical system are
absolutely essential for engaging with other people, and many
philosophical and theological systems place a heavy emphasis
on developing a healthy relationship between ourselves and
the broader world. If we define virtue as the excellence by
which we are perfectly realizing our soul's capacity, becoming more virtuous is also an offering that we can give to the
Gods, an intangible method of connecting our own partial

existence to their expansive, limitless oneness. This chapter approaches virtue from a summarizing introductory standpoint, with plenty of links. The goal is not to sell you on a specific system of virtue and ethics, but to familiarize you with the terrain and what you might look into on your own.

Many of us do not think about virtue, morality, or ethics constantly, at least until we are wronged by others or we need to make a hard decision between doing what is convenient and doing what is right. In Proclus' *Ten Problems Concerning Providence*, he writes (in alignment with Platonic teachings found in its texts like the *Phaedrus* and *Phaedo*) that virtue, and what we develop inwardly, remains with us through even the most extreme misfortunes (Proclus, 2012). We are often thwarted from achieving external delights, he says, but we can always turn inward to develop our inner core. In *On Providence*, Proclus expresses admiration for the teachings of Epictetus, especially the one on letting go of what we cannot control (Proclus, 2007). Plato himself in the *Phaedo* had Socrates say, "For the soul goes into Hades with nothing else except her education and nurture, which things are said to be of the greatest benefit or harm to the one who's met their end — right from the beginning of their journey There" (Plato, 1997: 107d). We carry our upbringing and what we learn with us as habitual and experiential imprints. Like a spiritual form of "you are what you eat," our goal is to develop frameworks, using the virtues as templates, for improving our inner state and bringing it in alignment with the Good.

We often think of virtue in terms of self-denial, with an image of a celibate monk or nun or other renunciate in our minds. Some of us think of something more sinister: the many horror movies set in Puritan-era New England or the exposés on unhealthy cults and the way that they obsessively control their members. The tension between embracing embodiment and fleeing from external pleasures has always existed, both in spiritual and secular philosophies and lifestyles. The guest-house metaphor I used for thinking about ancestry many chapters ago can also be used here as a bridge between this self-denying perspective and a perspective that embraces embodiment. Many virtue systems focus on correct behavior and action because we are acting out roles, and like actors in a play, taking too much of the role into ourselves can be destructive, especially if something happens that jars our most extreme negative emotions. In addition, without limits, we easily succumb to addictions and unhealthy patterns that we convince ourselves are freedoms, but which are actually ropes that bind us to specific pleasure-driven behaviors. We all occasionally struggle with negative self-talk and disappointment when we fail to live up to our best, and rather than punishing ourselves, we can use those moments as learning opportunities to inform how we behave in the future. Platonists like Damascius, Proclus, and Olympiodorus point out that many of the vices we have are coping mechanisms and "shortcuts" that we incorrectly assess will bring us happiness. Here is an example passage from Olympiodorus:

> And the pleasure-lover longs for divine ease, about which it has been said, 'the gods who live at ease' – that is the kind of idea that this person has in mind, but since he is unable to attain it, he fights over

shadows (*skiamakhein*), the reflections and expressions of this [higher idea]. And the money-lover longs for fulfilment and self-sufficiency, because self-sufficiency and fulfilment are divine — and so he desires this; but since he is unable to attain [the real thing], he grasps after it by loving money. And again, the reputation-lover longs for the god who is sufficient and freely giving, even if he is unable to attain this. (But being fulfilled (*teleion*) and being sufficient (*hikanon*) are not identical; for fulfilment is just needing nothing from another, whereas sufficiency is a matter not only of having no needs, but also being able to give freely to others (Olympiodorus, 2015:Lecture 5, 42–43).[1].

Here, what is interesting is the way Olympiodorus likens specific types of desires to our misapprehension that they will make us more like the Gods — in imitation of them, we reach for what is *not* them, and this leads us to a frustrating condition that in current times is known as hedonic adaptation. We will always be frustrated in our attempts to gain money, power, and pleasure, and we will always desire more; cultivating virtue and interrogating why we want what we want reduces the amount of suffering we experience. Giving in is like cutting off the heads of a hydra and thinking it's all taken care of only to see more grow instead of mindfully cauterizing the neck's stump.

Ethical guidance to follow may include things like the Delphic Maxims, Solon's Tenets, guidance within the Hávamál,

---

[1]All brackets from the translator.

Kemetic teachings on Ma'at, the Pythagorean Golden Verses, Stoic writings, Aristotle, the yamas and niyamas of yoga, and so on. There are often commentaries on these guidelines written by practitioners and academics. I encourage you to read as many systems as you need and to think about how they relate to your own life — many date back to ancient times, society has changed, and it can be useful to examine what has remained the same and what is different. The Delphic Maxims, as one example, include one that reads "rule your wife." Contextual to the culture at the time, men often married women much younger than them, most women did not enjoy vast personal freedoms, and the same stereotype existed about women being overindulgent spendthrifts that exists today in many parts of the world. The maxim is actually about ruling the parts of us that are less seasoned and more prone to desire, all bundled in a metaphor that many women have issues with when we read it.

In many cases, people will choose a system that is related to Gods they worship, especially since we have been habituated by the prevailing circumstances in America to view ethics as something given by religious tenets. At other times, it is more driven by philosophical school, regardless of the specific Gods someone worships. Once someone starts looking for other like-minded people, it is common for them to study a specific text or way of life together. In spiritual and religious organizations, learning a set of values may be part of the onboarding process.

One can even examine secular ethical and virtue writings, alone or in community, to tease apart the best elements of a virtuous life. This is especially true nowadays, as many philosophers, scholars, and public speakers who focus on virtue, ethics, and morality are writing from a nonreligious standpoint, albeit one informed by Christianity. This secular writing can be very helpful for reflecting on the values we learned as children in our society. Often, we pick up things without thinking deeply about them, and it's the process of reflection — on the sacred or the secular — that can truly help us become more excellent to one another.

7.1 A Continuous Process

Many people were taught in their childhood that missteps and incorrect behavior were shameful, often in ways that made them feel powerless to change how others had judged them. Some were even taught a particularly toxic form of either/or thinking — you are either virtuous and saved or twisted and damned. It is equally easy for people to react to an ethical system robotically, as if we are executing a computer program. First, we are not robots. Second, we must approach virtue and ethics from a growth mindset. We all start somewhere, and we all have aspects of our lives that we nail and other parts of our lives where we need to put in more work. This is true regardless of how embarrassed or ashamed we feel in the moments after we do something misguided or something awful happens to us. Gray areas will always challenge us to find solutions and stretch our abilities. While sometimes painful, we learn valuable lessons.

A growth mindset is adequately described in this passage

from Plotinus:

> If you do not yet see yourself as beautiful, then be
> like a sculptor who, making a statue that is sup-
> posed to be beautiful, removes a part here and
> polishes a part there so that he makes the latter
> smooth and the former just right until he has given
> the statue a beautiful face. In the same way, you
> should remove superfluities and straighten things
> that are crooked, work on the things that are dark,
> making them bright, and not stop 'working on your
> statue' until the divine splendour of virtue shines
> in you, until you see 'Self-Control enthroned on
> the holy seat (Plotinus, 2018: 1.6.9)

In the above passage, we are encouraged to actually work on
the parts of ourselves that seem daunting. From a practical
standpoint, we can ask ourselves:

- What are my unhealthy habits?

- What do I lie to myself about?

- What have I been avoiding?

- Last time I had a conflict with someone, what went
  wrong? Is there anything I need to learn for the next
  time I am in a similar situation?

- In the past, what has worked for me when my changing
  behavior? What hasn't worked?

- What are my strengths?

- How am I going to build self-care and self-compassion into my personal growth process?

The above questions may cause some distress, especially if we have been ignoring something for a long time. Look at pictures of cute animals, listen to relaxing music, and take care of yourself. Moral self-image stress can cause a lot of internal friction.

On a personal note, James Clear's *Atomic Habits*, Cal Newport's *Digital Minimalism*, the Fabulous App (see your device's app store), the *Daily Calm* meditation app, and the interpersonal trainings on LinkedIn Learning have all been immensely useful to me over the years. James Clear wrote, "You do not rise to the level of your goals. You fall to the level of your systems" (Clear, 2018). This has proven true for me, and it's one of the principles I used when describing how to start a prayer routine. The Fabulous App has helped me with procrastination and avoidance, two things I know I struggle with, by building better habits.

Do you need to talk to someone?

If you are experiencing mental health struggles, I encourage you to see a therapist. Talking through elements of our life with someone else can be a very valuable experience, especially for those of us who had rough childhoods and who developed toxic shame early in our lives. If your life feels overwhelming and you are considering an exit, please call the National Suicide Prevention Hotline at 800-273-8255.

7.1.1   Platonic Virtue

On a functional level, one of the reasons we have so many issues — at least in Platonism — is due to the operation of our three-part (tripartite) soul. As Plato's Socrates describes in the *Republic*, we have an appetitive soul (the seat of desire), described as many-headed; a spirited soul (the seat of emotional reactions), described as a lion; and the rational soul (the seat of our logical thinking), what makes us human. In embodiment, the soul's rational faculties are driven this way and that by the two layers of our irrational soul (appetitive and spirited). Many issues in life are due to not having a good handle on our impulses. The virtue that restrains the appetitive soul is temperance; the spirited soul, courage; and the rational soul, prudence. When everything is working together properly, the soul can manifest justice and its highest potential. Mishaps and brief falls are inevitable during our embodiment. If you fall off the bike, you get back on.

Platonism incorporates some elements from Aristotelian and Stoic teachings to classify levels of virtue according to nature, habitude (also called ethical), civic society, purificatory, contemplative, paradigmatic, and hieratic. Most people do not aim for the contemplative, paradigmatic, and hieratic virtues in their lives; to be functional members of society, we need to have everything up to the civic virtues nailed on a routine basis. The purificatory virtues signal a turn from that outer life to our own interior, culminating in the hieratic, which backflows outward from us and towards others through ritual action and care for the community. Tim Addey's *Unfolding Wings* discusses this in greater detail (Chapter 4), as does Mindy Mandell's *Discovering the Beauty of Wisdom* (Chapter 4) (Addey, 2011; Mandell, 2020). A good overview from an ancient commentator is Proclus' Essay 7 on the *Republic*, available in Volume II of a translated collection from Baltzly et al (Proclus, 2022). Proclus and Olympiodorus also focus on virtue in their commentaries on *Alcibiades I*. The translator of Olympidorus' commentary on *Alcibiades I* did a video presentation on the Platonic ladder of virtue (Griffin, Michael, 2020). Mindy Mandell's YouTube channel about Platonism includes several videos that walk through her teaching lineage's position on limiting beliefs and how to overcome them, including the videos "All About Platonism: Purification" and "The Philosopher's Journey" on a playlist of practical advice.[2]

Usually, the things we want to work on are bad habits. Occasionally, we have errors in our civic judgments — our sense of what is politically right and wrong may be off. Sometimes, we cannot handle our cognitive dissonance because it gives us pain. If we gather our courage, confront that dissonance, and overcome it, we may reactively seek out the first ideology that seems "correct" and that soothes our feelings of pain about our past judgment mistakes. This perpetuates the cycle of ignorance. It is better to explore *what* was wrong about our old beliefs and to critically interrogate every system we approach — to think for ourselves. We want to catch a glimpse of Justice Itself, and we want to see how the Form of Justice breaks upon the bodies of the worlds to en-form what is around us. This is the only way to make our civic and political environment better. Tim Addey wrote, strikingly, that "conflicting temper-

---

[2]https://www.youtube.com/playlist?list=PLoPggAqEExYbxQktPv8 XGWm2bnPXUnuZw

aments are often harmonized and reconciled by communal forces [at the habitual level], and [they] only reemerge during the breakdown of civil order" (Addey, 2011: 67). I often think about that when I look at the major political upheavals we experience today and how chaotically people react to them.

Virtue has a direct connection to our capacity to receive the Gods when we pray. Working on it calms the discord within our heads. It pulls the soul back from the many desires and passions into unity. It soothes those constant inner voices and feelings and the whirlpool of anxieties we feel. It teaches us the difference between what we must accept and what we can act on. When we are calm inside, we can more easily focus when we pray, and we are not wasting valuable cognitive energy, so we can be more effective people. In the *Laws*, Plato writes:

> [T]he finest and truest of all principles, in my view — which is that for the good person, in the natural order of things, sacrifice to the gods, contact with them by means of prayers and offerings, and religious observance of every kind is at all times finest and best, the most likely to result in a happy life, and far and away the most appropriate thing for [a person] (Plato, 2016: 716d).

7.2   Exercise: Self-Compassion Meditation

Self-compassion meditations are everywhere. As someone who does not teach meditation, this exercise has three components:

1. Locate a self-compassion meditation.

2. Do the meditation.

3. If you like the meditation, do it for a few weeks — pick the date, time, and place you will do this. If you don't like the meditation, try another kind of self-compassion meditation until you find one that works for you.

When thinking about where we fall short of an ideal, all too often, we judge ourselves with more harshness than we deserve. Some of us may even shut down and think, "Well, if I'm not perfect, or with the background I have, what is even the point?" Cultivating self-compassion blunts the impact of these feelings and helps us remain grounded in our inner goodness and potential to be better people.

When you locate a compassion meditation, try to figure out what the meditation is asking you to do. Compassion meditations that ask me to think of a nice thing I have done for someone else make me confused and worried. The first time I tried it, I failed to think of anything, so I looked online to see what people meant. It turned out that many people classify behaviors as "nice" that I was taught were basic courtesy. Even at work, my job is focused on helping people find what they need, so giving a stranger my time and attention is part of a normal day. I have more success with the type of compassion meditation in which one imagines feelings of goodwill and lovingkindness towards others. Some meditations ask us to visualize receiving love from someone who cares about us. I usually think of a God during those segments.

If you use Headspace, there is a self-compassion course in

the app by Dora Kamau; she also has a website and a presence on the Insight Timer app. The Headspace course uses my favorite type of compassion exercise. Other meditation apps (such as Calm) will show you what is available after doing a keyword search. Dr. Kristin Neff, a researcher who does significant work on self-compassion, has free downloadable meditations on her website.[3]

7.3   Exercise: Contemplate Ethical Guidance

During this contemplation exercise, find some time when you will not be disturbed for a few minutes. Find a pen and paper to write down any thoughts that come up.

Begin this exercise with a prayer to the God(s) of your choice. Then, read aloud the following:

> Put more trust in nobility of character than in an oath. Never tell a lie. Pursue worthy aims. Do not be rash to make friends and, when once they are made, do not drop them. Learn to obey before you command. In giving advice seek to help, not to please, your friend. Be led by reason. Shun evil company. Honour the gods, reverence parents (Laërtius, 1925).

Taking each sentence on its own, what comes up for you? Where in your life do you display the value expressed in this tenet? Where could you invest more work, and how?

---

[3]https://insighttimer.com/dorakamau
https://self-compassion.org/guided-self-compassion-meditations-mp3-2/

Do this for each of the elements in turn. When done, thank the God(s) and use the document you have created to create actionable plans for self-development. Feel free to move on to investigate other ethical texts and repeat this exercise. Usually, you will want to reflect on a small chunk of the material.

Chapter 8

Navigating Groups

A *group* is any collection of people, whether it has convened informally or formally. It could be your family, people you've met online, or a few people in town with whom you get drinks and catch up. It could also be your team at work, the members of an organization, or those on the membership rolls of a specific religion or who attend events associated with a spiritual group.

In this chapter, we will discuss groups, both in a general sense and in terms of what you need to check on to avoid cults and toxic people. What I have to say in this chapter is informed by the realities of the social media era, a time in which we are more connected than we have ever been in human history, yet feel more alone and isolated (Jarzyna, 2021). Having a supportive, solid group of people to bounce ideas off of and who can come together for rituals, virtual or in-person, is a wonderful thing that can supplement one's at-home practice.

Homo sapiens sapiens is a species that evolved to be most at ease in tribal bands of 50-200 people. We need other people for psychological safety, well-being, and a sense of belonging. We have trouble with groups larger than that because our brains struggle with depersonalizing others. Even the most introverted person wants to feel a sense of respect and care from people in their immediate community. In a spiritual sense, it can be good to have family and friends to decompress with about spiritual issues and with whom you can celebrate larger holidays, and it is vital for checks and balances to have level-headed elders and friends who can give both critical and supportive feedback.

About this chapter's focus ...

This chapter focuses on groups and spiritual friendships in a broad sense. *Out-of-scope* is any group that is centered around a temple for one or more Gods. Those groups are service-oriented — in this practice, a community comes into being around a God and expresses its spiritual development through the commitment of time, resources, (usually) permanent property reserved for the God(s), and festivals. This formal spiritual service involves a lot of ego sacrifice and cultivation of self-discipline. What I have written about avoiding toxic groups, modern cults, and harmful leaders still applies, but since the focus is on the community and its rituals for the God(s), some of what I say about prioritizing yourself and your own practice applies less. You should still check its articles of incorporation and rules to ensure that the God is prioritized over the leaders.

Jean-Paul Sartre wrote that Hell is other people, and to a certain extent, that is true (Rugnetta and Brown, 2014). In the piece I just cited, the writer explains that it's not because people irritate us and we have painful interpersonal drama, but because we are judged and judge in social situations. We can be both the victims of cruelty and the ones who mete it out.

Now, in the context of many Gods, there is no hell that directly corresponds to the Christian one — for example, the closest in the belief system I follow would be Tartarus, which is where souls that have made many bad decisions in their most recent life are purified. (Imagine if you were put in a room with a firm, yet compassionate, therapist-judge and couldn't leave until you'd worked through all you had going on in your last life. To call that *rough* is an understatement.) Other belief systems have similar states of being. The point, however, is that we can be awful to one another. Sometimes this awfulness arises out of ignorance or obliviousness. At other times, someone wants to gain status and is willing to lie to get it. We can also get so caught up in the storylines of our embodied lives that we become unwilling to budge; on the flip side, we can challenge unhealthy dynamics, ideas, or behaviors and have what we thought were steady relationships blow up in our faces.

8.1   Family

I am very lucky in that I grew up praying to mother Goddesses in the backwoods. I was with my family and in a very loose community. We went to a Unitarian Society many Sundays, although the religious education program for kids was often more miss than hit, but the true joys were when we convened every six weeks at some family friends' rural property and were able to process to a sacred place, do ritual, and have a potluck in community afterward. We celebrated the seasons, the elements, a God, and a Goddess.

My parents never required that my sisters and I participate, and we rarely did family rituals at home, but they were very open that we *could* participate. I am a self-directed, "okay, let's do this" person when it comes to spirituality, and I always have been. The Christian denominations we were in when I was a very young child made no sense, and when we apostatized, I was relieved because the framework of many Gods felt right, and I was happy we had ended up in something that made more logical sense. Later on, when I became interested in theology, my feelings became grounded in something more. My youngest sister rebelled against the family by getting interested in very conservative Christianity as a teen, although that didn't last. My middle sister felt that she wasn't included in the family rituals and that it was "our thing" — for our parents and me. I only learned this after we were all adults and she discussed wanting to go deeper into the practice. It made me feel awful that I hadn't been there for her.

Based on comparing our childhood experiences, I do recommend involving your kids — if you can — in revering many Gods. Let them *know* that they're welcome, explain why you pray to the Gods you pray to and that they can to pray to whomever they like, and be open to their participation in your daily rituals if they want that. If they say no, have them participate in holidays, but don't force them to do more. If they want a sacred space in their rooms, help them. I started using candles in my room when I was twelve, at about the same age I started doing my family's laundry and much of the weeknight cooking. You know your children and their maturity level. Depending on your kids and their engagement with large media franchises, you may have to explain how worshipping Greek deities is different from Percy Jackson (the "chosenness" thing can be particularly tricky for kids; I remember encountering a bunch of teens once who thought they were demigod children of deities because they'd fallen into that extreme escapist belief online) or how the Marvel characters named for Norse Gods are just imaginative interpretations of myth created by screenwriters who are mostly atheists.

On Devices

Make sure that, to the extent possible, any shared family ritual time is a device-free zone. It's OK to use eReaders, computers, or phones to access texts, show sacred images, or use a playlist. Just make sure that any device is silenced or in airplane mode and that only the apps you need are open.

Sometimes, a person starts following many Gods after a period of significant trauma in their early religious life, such as those who left cults. Emphasizing participation in spirituality or even teaching a child ethics can bring up feelings about what happened when the parent was younger. Keep in mind that your child may have no idea, or only a vague idea, of what happened to you. Shield them from your experience by modeling the values that you want them to have when they grow up. Emphasize ethics, but be sure to focus on a growth mindset in which we as individuals are continuously learning to be better people, not one in which small mistakes are damning. If you can, consider seeing an individual or family therapist.

Finally, involving your kid comes with some important safety tips. To be blunt, your child will go online — either with your permission or in secret. What you want is for your child to have a firm foundation in reality so they don't end up joining a cult or some fringe group that believes it is channeling new physics from aliens on a planet orbiting Zeta Reticuli. Critical thinking skills are an absolute must. Teach your kids how to distinguish among religion, mystical/esoteric practices, New Age, and the occult. New Age is where many of the fringe beliefs are, but fringe can spill over into the other communities I just mentioned — and, when we think of modern conspiracy phenomena, it is very clear that no segment of the population is wholly immune. Developing a firm foundation can be challenging for children who have a score of four or higher on ACE (Adverse Child Experiences) tests, which correlates with higher chances of self-soothing escapism and failure to thrive as adults. I have an ACE score of four, and I held some embarrassing beliefs in my late teens that developed as coping mechanisms. It wasn't until going to therapy in my late 20s and graduating from therapy after getting very into Platonism and learning growth-based frames for thinking about myself and my life experiences that I started to feel steady.

Even when something a child encounters online is sound, there is so much overlap online among pagans, polytheists, and indigenous traditions, on the one hand, and the occult and witchcraft on the other, that it becomes easy to confuse these communities. Online, we are all exposed to new ideas from people with backgrounds that are completely unfamiliar to us, good and bad. *The Soul's Inner Statues* is emphasizing a theistic, many-Gods approach. It is not connected to witchcraft or the occult — and if the approach that I am presenting is what you are most comfortable with, keep the "we worship many Gods" identity at your heart when you and your kids go online. If you want to do magic or occult practices, be clear to your child what is your core spiritual practice and what you're doing in addition to it. If they grow up and enjoy praying a bit, but don't like magic, this helps them make good decisions about what to include or exclude from their spiritual practice without thinking that it's an all-or-nothing situation.

Kids don't need to be watched every second they're connected to the web, but they do need structure, critical thinking, and parents who care about their spiritual lives. They need to be taught what boundaries are. They can be given greater and greater responsibility over their own spiritual growth as they develop from babies to teens to adults.

8.2   Partners and Roommates

If you have other adults in your living space, like a spouse or roommate, involving them in your religion could take several forms. If the other adult also worships many Gods (likely different ones), holidays in your respective traditions are opportunities to share food and stories and pray together. If your spouse or roommates are not religious, they may also be perfectly fine with sharing a special meal for holidays — most nonreligious people and atheists are not antireligious even if YouTube comments and online trolls indicate otherwise.

If your spouse or roommate is antireligious, you will likely experience substantial friction. Members of exclusivist monotheistic faiths who are progressive may also be willing to have meals with you, but more conservative ones will likely have issues with you and call you an idolater. I know someone whose spouse believes she is consorting with demons, and it's psychologically hard for her as someone who is drawn to worshipping other Gods to have her spouse be that hostile.

8.3 Finding People

This section relies on three words for nonromantic, non-kin interpersonal relationships: parasociality, acquaintanceship, and friendship. In the United States, many people will not distinguish between acquaintances and friends, but I find that this is a crucial frame to help me calibrate my social obligations towards others, especially as someone who was not trained to have good empathic boundaries as a child.

Parasocial is a term developed in the mid-1950s to describe the relationship between TV personalities and their audiences (Hoffner and Bond, 2022). In the early days of the social media era, Influencers began using it to describe their relationships with the massive numbers of people who interact with them.

More recently, it has begun to refer to interactions among people who really don't know each other online — you follow their content, they follow yours, but you two do not interact as either acquaintances or friends. In a parasocial relationship, we typically have one-sided information about someone. Online, we share carefully-curated details about our lives, so much so that others feel they know and trust us when they may have only a vague idea of who we even are, if any idea at all. It plays with the follower's emotions and may lead to feelings of devotion, allegiance, goodwill, betrayal, moral outrage, and social rejection, as mercurial as a stormy sea, based on what someone posts. While most of us do not have a huge online reach, Influencers and celebrities do, and they experience the downsides of parasocial relationships more intensely than the rest of us.

Acquaintanceship is a mutual state in which you vaguely know someone, but may not be on the same page about who both of you are. More distant acquaintances are people who see each other and say hi at the gym, while catching transit, or when chatting on discussion fora or chat servers. Close acquaintances are people who have decided that they care about each other in a vague social sense, enough to have genuine interest in how things are going. Perhaps they learn the names of one another's pets or children or even share phone numbers or start emailing. The mutuality is key here — whereas in a parasocial relationship, you are engaging with someone's broadcasted content, in an acquaintanceship, you are actually getting to know each other. Many acquaintances are perfectly happy not to have a deeper level of engagement. Aristotle, while he had a dubious understanding of the Platonic Forms and an irritating lack of respect for women, has a lot of really useful perspective in the *Nichomachean Ethics* (chapters 8 and 9) for thinking about friendship. He describes something called a "friendship based on utility" that "belongs to the marketplace" (Aristotle, 2012:1158a, 21–23). Utilitarian friendships, in my opinion, are professional, collegial, or logistical close acquaintanceships.

The pathway from acquaintanceship to friendship involves gradual steps, usually in the form of mutual experiences. People seeking to make friends will also start to disclose more information, gradually testing the waters to see if the feelings of affinity are reciprocated and if the other party can be trusted.

Friendship, like acquaintanceship, comes in layers. Casual friends care about one another, take interest in one another's lives, and may have some shared values in common. They may also be members of a social cluster who are more peripheral to each other than to others in the group, or they may have become friends due to shared professional or personal experiences. Friendship of this nature is also friendship between those who are prepared to be mutual and who see one another at (roughly) the same level — as equals — even if there are differences in age, social class, or cultural background. The "purification of correction" (a concept that the ancient Platonists sometimes discuss), or the mutual checks friends offer one another, is possible at this level of interaction because friends generally want what is best for one another and care enough to allow the other to be imperfect, and friends care enough to correct one another tactfully.

Aristotle writes that "a wish for friendship arises swiftly, but friendship itself does not" (Aristotle, 2012:1156b, 30). This is true in both the transition of acquaintances to friends and about the transition from casual to close friends. While in a casual friendship, one might censor oneself and keep some things private, *close* friends generally share much more of themselves with one another. Aristotle calls this form of friendship *complete friendship* (Aristotle, 2012:1156b, 5) — the two of you have similar grasps of virtue and enough similarity in outlook that you can know and accept one another's character. A person cannot sustain many of these relationships at once.

Friendship is where ethical imperatives towards one's associates appear in full force — Solon's ethical tenets instruct us to be slow in making friends, but not to abandon them once we have solidified our friendship. That makes the most sense when applied to friends who are at middle to total levels of closeness. Aristotle provides guidance on this, too, in the *Nicomachean Ethics*, saying that corruptions of virtue and outlook among our close friends must be approached with care for their character, not out of interest in their public persona or property or the utilitarian benefits of the friendship. Even when a friendship cannot be maintained, he writes that "on account of their prior friendship, [we must] render something to those who were once friends, when its dissolution was not due to excessive corruption" (Aristotle, 2012:1165b, 35). Ending a close friendship is a last resort. And trust me: If one of your friends, medium-close or close, gets cancelled or doxxed by parasocials, you will feel the heat from this, and the parasocials will assume you have no moral backbone and are willing to just chuck your friend to the curb at the drop of a hat. Come to a decision about the friendship on your own.

While in a parasocial relationship, the feelings of betrayal have no actual basis in mutual care, feelings of betrayal and hurt when something bad happens in a casual-to-close friendship are based on a real connection. They can often be resolved by actually talking it out with the friend. Unlike with children, irreversible fallouts rarely happen at the drop of a hat. You can be more of your whole self with close friends without fearing that they will turn on you or that their care is conditional. Often, those of us who have spent some time on social media can harbor a lot of anxiety about being fully open and vulnerable around friends, as we see so much toxic behavior. In my experience, the toxic behavior is most likely to happen with acquaintances and friends who are seeking social status and validation and who have done this to others before. We can rationalize seeing them do this and assume it will never happen to us, but this is a red flag.

Many of us also tend to learn ethical frameworks fairly late in childhood or young adulthood, so we may have associations with people that are misguided or situations that we were never mentored to navigate by our elders. If you need to exit any associations like that, do have compassion for yourself and the other party or parties. Do not cling to bitter things from chapters of your life that have concluded.

I started this section with an overview of friendships for one key reason: **Just because others worship Gods, and even**

the same Gods as you, doesn't mean you'll all get along. This is a painful life lesson. Our personalities are all unique, no matter how we try to bin them into categories with Myers-Briggs, astrology, or anything else. One might think that being in the series of the same God, if two people were to be blessed with confident insight into that, would make them instant friends. Even in that case, since a God is everything in a unique way, and as each of us is a particular soul that expresses a unique fingerprint of that uniqueness, devotees express the full range of who and what that God is.

Ideally, when looking for people to approach about your mutual interest in the Gods, your goal is to identify candidates for close acquaintances and casual friends. Rarely, you will develop new close friends.

8.3.1   Local Organizations

Depending on the size and demographics of your local area, there may be people nearby with preexisting groups that you can join. Shops that sell "alternative" religious materials (like incense, deity statues, and so on) often have good inventories of the groups that exist nearby. You can use Meetup or Eventbrite and check for groups on social media that are local. Many will have some public events even if their core activities are private and members-only.

If you are worshipping deities that have temples or shrines in your metro area, learn more about the organizations around you and contact them to ask if it is possible for you to pray there. Generally speaking, they will have volunteers and other people who would be happy to show a respectful outsider how to engage with the Gods in a tactful manner.

8.3.2 Social Media

To find friends in the 2020s, most people start on social media platforms, Influencer-related Discord or Slack servers, and Internet forums. There are some important pitfalls, and I advise you to use social media strategically to identify people you actually want to talk to. Once you have that, get out. Especially in private Discords that are run by Influencer personalities (which I recommend avoiding), things can quickly go south into cult-land. Discord servers that are *not* related to an Influencer, that have clear rules about cults of personality, and that host level-headed discussion among equals are less of an issue — they're more like going to your local pub or coffeehouse.

The reason I encourage you to have an exit game is that the psychological impacts of heavy social media use are similar to other high-risk addictive behaviors. Once you feel parasocially obligated to be online and post to a large audience, you will also likely be "trapped" on whatever platform you're using. Studies show that people who are primarily active on social media for their social interaction face higher rates of anxiety and depression, as social media doses us with dopamine using algorithms similar to casino slot machines. Parasocial validation cannot functionally replace getting to know people privately. Unfortunately, many of us are also lonely and lack robust in-person networks, so social media is used as a stand-in (Jarzyna, 2021; Valkenburg, 2022; Meshi and Ellithorpe, 2021).

While you are on social media, be it TikTok, Facebook,

Twitter, or the latest and greatest new platform, do not feel pressure to follow back or friend anyone. Your update feed is your space. Look at the person's profile and decide if you find their updates parasocially relevant. If so, follow. If not, don't. When I was very active on social media, I rarely followed back immediately — and it often took me weeks, months, or years to do so. Most people I followed were writing content that I found useful or whose updates I'd be looking up using the search function. In private social media spaces, I only let people see my content if I feel comfortable having them see it. Occasionally, I follow people back when I already know them (distant to close acquaintances). One rarely knows why someone is following the people they follow. Knowing a stranger's habits that well is a bit creepy.

Facebook groups and Instagram hashtags about the Gods are also filled with what I like to call aesthetic posts — people posing with animal skins, horns, period clothing, and other items. It is materialistic and annoying for people who are actually there for content that helps them grow spiritually. It can also trigger our acquisitive instincts due to the human instinct to conform to group norms. Even when people post shrine photos, it can prompt a materialistic impulse for people whose setups are simpler and less expensive. Unless you know someone, you have no idea if they've been practicing for 20 years and have built their shrine items up over that amount of time or if they went into debt buying all of those items two months ago. Shrine photos are fine, though, when they give you ideas for what you can do with the space that you have.

Social media rewards oversharing, negative content, and

a lack of personal filter/boundaries. For this reason, spiritual bypassing, out-of-the-norm experiences, and misinformation are all rewarded by the algorithms. Rather than sit with a private experience for a while, many people instantly share what they think happened with strangers online. Sharing personal experiences is best done first in a private journal, then among people one actually knows and trusts. Because many of us are lonely and lack close friends, social media oversharing becomes even more seductive. We are all more likely to post when we are feeling strong emotions, too, like when online misinformation pushes our buttons. We all slip up.

If you are on social media for personal or professional reasons, remember that when fights happen on social media, most people in the conversations are fighting with shadows created by their own fears, not with you. This is why people can get so vindictive — the depersonalization involved in online interactions combines with whatever is going on in their mental and emotional landscape to make a bad situation even worse. If you have learned techniques from difficult conversations trainings (my workplace has these all the time), now is the time to use them. Over the years, I have learned that it is impossible to deescalate everything, even with training. Some fires are just not containable.

8.4 The Mechanics of Group Ritual

Once you find one or more people to do ritual with, it's time to look at your longer ritual outlines. Typically, whether you do a ritual in-person or on a digital platform like Zoom, you will need to share the ritual outline ahead of time. If everyone involved worships many Gods, there may be edits and amendments based on elements of practice that others want to include. Google Docs or another multi-person editing tool is great for this.

Collaboratively assign people roles. When I was growing up, we knew that the hosts who owned the property would be managing the overall ritual, but they took volunteers for invoking the elements and the ritual's deities. This happened when people were gathering in the processional area about ten minutes before the ritual started. If you know who will attend your rituals beforehand, in Google Drive or another collaboration tool, let people pick which sections of the ritual they want to take charge of.

If running a ritual on Zoom or another videoconferencing platform, be sure that someone is taking the role of Zoom host — this person can spotlight the person doing each part of the ritual. Chanting isn't as easy on Zoom as it is in person, so you may want to mute everyone except the chant leader. Be clear with everyone whether you are all doing the ritual simultaneously together (with similar offerings and space setups) or if one person will show the ritual setup and make the offerings. If it's the latter, the designated ritual space provider should be spotlighted even when others are speaking.

Some groups will do a debrief of the entire ritual immediately before the ritual takes place, which can be tedious for those who came prepared. I recommend doing this offline and setting an expectation that everyone is reading through the materials in advance. If new people are present who are unfamiliar, do not assign them anything, but make sure you or another person welcomes them and is available to answer any questions after the ritual.

Most often, people will use their own homes for rituals and trust that guests will follow rules of hospitality. They may also secure permits to do rituals in public spaces like parks if the ritual is large enough; if it's only a few people, they might just go to the park, depending on local regulations. Less frequently, groups may rent a space (a Unitarian Universalist Church is great for that), which can help establish trust among people who don't know one another well enough to feel okay sharing their home address yet. Within traditions that worship many Gods, there are sometimes physical locations that are supported by the community, either temples or land.

8.5   Joining Groups

So, let's say that you decide you like a group — online or offline — and want to be a joiner. Congratulations on having taken such a big step! You're going to learn a lot, and I hope that this primer has been helpful.

When you are making your decision, here are some things to look for, but this is not a checklist — the most important things are that the group encourages mutual respect and spiritual growth.

1. Does the group have a nondiscrimination policy? How is it enforced? Is training mandatory for officers? Many are quick to sign statements about inclusivity, but few

are willing to put in the work to ensure that leaders are actually prepared to handle conflict situations.

2. Is the group centered around a single person? If it is centered around one person, is it because they have the highest level of training in the tradition? Who trained them? Is there an accountability structure that applies to people with their level of training at the regional, national, or international level? How are officers and leaders of the group chosen?

3. Has the group appeared in the news associated with any cult scandals? Have former members written any exposés? What did they say, and how did the group respond?

4. If the group is claiming to be a revival of a tradition from a region, are people who are descendants of the group(s) living in that region represented in leadership positions — and not just in a tokenizing fashion? Thinking back to the cultural appropriation content earlier in this book, is the group engaging in any red flags? What do members of the group say about the tradition's living descendants in general? Is the group open to growth and change, or does it fall under "reenactment"?

5. If you have children, is the group child-friendly? Are there some rituals that are fine for the whole family and others that are restricted to teens and adults? Is there childcare? If nobody has kids, this isn't an issue, but it may become one.

6. What are the educational development opportunities

for members?

7. Is the group legally incorporated? This isn't a dealbreaker, but groups that have legally incorporated are often more stable than ones that are not. Decentralized continuous traditions may not be incorporated, so this question does not apply to them.

Using these questions to frame your research, you should be prepared to sift through the organization's website and ask questions of members of the group if you attend a few rituals and want to know more about them. I was once in a group where long-term members repeatedly described, in an elated way, how they thought outsiders would go after them if they were successful and how they were prepared for the worst. Red flags like that will likely not be on the website — you have to get to know people.

Once you have found a group, sign up for its listservs, forums, and other online presence locations. Try to make at least a few of their in-person or online meetups when possible. When I first joined one group, I lurked for a long time, but it meant that I didn't get a feel for what other people in the group were like until I was eligible for leadership positions, and I came to know that we did not have compatible values.

8.5.1 When Leaders Go Bad

Throughout our youths, we come to know that the authority figures in our lives — our parents, other adults, religious teachers, and so on — are just as human and fallible as we are. The first time I saw someone I considered a spiritual leader behave in a toxic way online, I was in my early 20s. Nowadays, with the way social media is designed, I imagine people have this shock at a much younger age. When I saw what I saw, I was only *witnessing* what was happening, and I still had to process extreme disappointment.

Unfortunately, that experience is mild in comparison to what happens to many other people. Cults, sexual abuse, and similar horrors are rampant in interpersonal spaces, spiritual or secular. These things may be centered around a specific person, or they may take place within the context of a group's organizational structure.

When it comes to individuals, we can draw some understanding from the commentary that Edwin F. Bryant made on Patañjali's *Yoga Sūtras*. In a chapter on meditative absorption, Bryant translates I.15 as, "Dispassion is the controlled consciousness of one who is without craving for sense objects, whether these are actually perceived or described" (Bryant, 2009: 52). He cites two prior commentators on the same passage of the *Yoga Sūtras*: dispassion is "indifference to objects even when these are available" (Vācaspati Miśra) and includes "members of the opposite sex, food, drink, and power" (Vyāsa). This echoes things said in Platonism about control of the passions of the appetitive and spirited parts of the human soul, which — when they are left unchecked because someone has not properly brought them into alignment — lead to disasters great and small. "The wise," Bryant continues, "strive for detachment and the eternal experience of the soul rather than the never-ending pursuit of ephemeral pleasure" (Bryant, 2009: 53).

It is that detachment that allows someone to lead a group without being corrupted by power — and, crucially, even when someone starts out holy, they can backslide. Spiritual teachers are honestly some of the most vulnerable people to lies, tyrannical downfalls, vice, and abuse, partially because people trust them, and we are less likely to hold people we admire accountable. The goal of being a guide for others is to positively impact others' minds and souls, and those others then open up and become vulnerable. Socrates gets into how devastating spiritual abuse can be at *Phaedo* 89d-e, as it hardens people against any spirituality or truth-seeking at all — the wound leaves them jaded. A spiritual teacher needs a group of peers and friends to hold them accountable, people who are not afraid to say the hard things.

In the same commentary on the *Yoga Sūtras*, at I.14 ("practice becomes firmly established when it has been cultivated uninterruptedly and with devotion over a prolonged period of time" (Bryant, 2009: 49)), Bryant takes what Patañjali has written to comment on the recent stream of abuse scandals in yoga. According to him, the practice must be cultivated continuously, like a garden. Otherwise, disaster may happen:

> As an aside, many Hindu gurus and yogīs have been embroiled in scandals that have brought disrepute to the transplantation of yoga and other Indic spiritual systems to the West. This sūtra provides a mechanism of interpreting such occurrences. If one reads the early hagiographies of many Hindu gurus whose integrity was later found compromised, one is struck by the intensity, de-

votedness, and accomplishments of their initial practices. Nonetheless, however accomplished a yogī may become, if he or she abandons the practice of yoga under the notion of being enlightened or of having arrived at a point beyond the need of practice, it may be only a matter of time before past saṁskāras, including those of past sensual indulgences, now unimpeded by practice, begin to surface. The result is scandal and traumatized disciples. There is no flower bed, however perfected, that can counteract the relentless emergence of weeds if left unattended. As Patañjali will discuss later in the text, as long as one is embodied, saṁskāras remain latent, and therefore potential, in the citta [mind]. Hence one can read this sūtra as indicating that since the practices of yoga must be uninterrupted, one would be wise to politely avoid yogīs or gurus who claim to have attained a state of enlightenment such that they have transcended the need for the practice and renunciation presented by Patañjali here (Bryant, 2009: 51).

This passage could apply to any spiritual community: The leaders cannot, for the sake of those following them, fall prey to power. Sometimes, people go into leadership positions because they feel a lack that they believe only power over others can provide, and they spend the remainder of their lives hiding skeletons in their closets and using their current followers as a replacement for real self-improvement. Leadership often ends badly for them. In any case, the fallout impacts the entire group. It is negligence at its best, calculated indifference to the welfare of others at its worst. All teachers need training and accountability. All teachers need to demonstrate care towards the souls of others, imitating the Gods, as the Gods are wholly good. If an asteroid impacted Earth tomorrow and wiped our species out, does being the leader of a group matter as much as helping others get started with their own relationship with the Gods? We cannot take awards or good reviews with us. We are seeded from a variety of Gods, with diverse dispositions, and the personal, private practices we cultivate for ourselves are what is most vital.

Beyond leaders and teachers, toxic groups scare people with what will happen to them. They ostracize someone who criticizes a group policy instead of inviting discussion, explanations, and (perhaps) change. They terrorize people if they make simple human mistakes. They judge and punish if a member likes the wrong books, buys food out-of-line with the group's norms, or displays negative emotions (Montell, 2021). Meanwhile, they puff up followers with the idea that they are members of a special, awakened elite. You cannot be compassionate or cultivate civic virtue if you internalize us/them exclusivity rhetoric.

Often, those drawn into a cult are people who are motivated to do good in the world — just as Plato teaches, people always want to do what they think is best, even if they are in error. Their strong motivation to do good is manipulated through love-bombing and the fear of ostracism and hatred from the people they respect. Us/them thinking and "we're

the only good people and you must believe these specific doctrines, and these alone" rhetoric is extremely prevalent in
online New Religious Movement communities in the 2020s,
on the right and the left. Do not trust people who try to cut
you off from different ideas while threatening to ostracize you
if you disobey.

Paradoxically, the language of "we're a niche" is also used
in a less intense way in nontoxic systems. In Platonism, for
example, theurgic and philosophical incarnation choices are
prioritized for achieving henosis and a providential exit from
the current cosmic cycle. But it encourages critical thinking
at the same time — you are supposed to question, to work
through the dialogues, to understand that even the holiest
people incarnated were human beings. Exegesis is a torch
relay. When people try to misapply Platonism for spiritual
bypassing or to gain power, they will often be overly literal in
interpreting texts and/or fuse Platonism with a prevailing political current or zeitgeist, and they will miss the interpretive
mark.

Be wary of leaders who try to twist your embodiment anxiety and desire for transcendence into something toxic to your
soul. Be wary of leaders who plaster their faces everywhere —
while dead holy people are honored with libations and appropriate commemorative well-wishes, human beings, dead or
alive, should not be revered as if they are of the same status
as the Gods — and those who scare you into silence with the
threat of ostracism if you question anything or have slightly
different beliefs than they do.

The Gods are the wellsprings of human happiness, as per

Iamblichus. Humans swim in an ocean of transient pleasures and pains. Follow the Gods, and they will lead you up the mountain to touch the sky. Follow humans uncritically, and they may very well lead you to the bottom of an ocean trench.

8.6 Exercise: Know What You Want

Research groups, either tradition-specific or not, based on who you worship and what you are looking for in a community. Use the questions above and narrow down to one or two (if possible) to learn more about. Try attending one of the group's open events if you can.

Meanwhile, identify what you want in online or in-person spiritual friends. What are the values you are looking for in someone else? Your dealbreakers? Where do you plan to meet people? If you plan to use social media, what rules do you want to set around using the platform?

These questions are ideal for answering in a journal or text file, and you can refer back to them over the next few months. I recommend checking in about your social media habits at least monthly to ensure that you are not succumbing to overuse.

Chapter 9

Conclusion

We started off this primer by talking about the Gods and introducing ourselves to them. In only a few chapters, we went through a whirlwind of information about getting started with a ritual practice, all framed as an uncovering of our soul's inner statues and our relationship to the Gods who are the root of us all.

It goes without saying that all spiritual practices are iterative — a process of listening to the Gods and to our own inner voice, a conversation and a dance. There are things I do now that I did not do when I was twenty; there are things I will do at fifty that I do not do now in my thirties. The same is true for all of us. Some of my practices changed dramatically while writing this book as I puzzled through the best way to say things and thought hard about the implications of what I had to offer to you, practitioner-to-practitioner.

I wish you all of the blessings, luck, and divine guidance that the Gods can give you. I will close with words from Iamblichus.

Extended practice of prayer nurtures our intellect, enlarges very greatly our soul's receptivity to the gods, reveals to [people] the life of the gods, accustoms their eyes to the brightness of divine light, and gradually brings to perfection the capacity of our faculties for contact with the gods, until it leads us up to the highest level of consciousness (of which we are capable); also, it elevates gently the dispositions of our minds, and communicates to us those of the gods, stimulates persuasion and communion and indissoluble friendship, augments divine love, kindles the divine element in the soul, scours away all contrary tendencies within it, casts out from the aetherial and luminous vehicle surrounding the soul everything that tends to generation, brings to perfection good hope and faith concerning the light; and, in a word, it renders those who employ prayers, if we may so express it, the familiar consorts of the gods (Iamblichus, 2003: V.26).

Chapter 10

Acknowledgments and Next-Step Reads

10.1 Acknowledgments

When I started praying to Bast at the age of nine, and at ten when my parents first brought me to Circle, the world was very different. As a kid, my dad would take me to the mall. I would usually end up in Waldenbooks, where I perused the spirituality section (all four shelves) and the discount books on display at the front of the store. My mother would take me to the Opened Book in Hannibal, MO, where I purchased ritual supplies and pagan books.

As most children do, I acquired most of those early items by pleading; when I was 15 and able to work, I used my pocket money. The community in the Hannibal, MO, area was the best thing that happened to me as a child, a bright star. I dearly hope that everyone who knew me as a child, teen, and young adult forgives my embarrassing flaws and accepts my gratitude. I am extremely thankful for the communities of affinity I have fallen into over the past few years — while many have lamented the pandemic for a lack of closeness, Zoom has brought me to so many amazing people and meaningful discussions. Co-reading Platonic texts with other people is such a world-changing experience. You know who you are if you are reading this. I also acknowledge my more recent interlocutors on the blogosphere and other text-based online venues — we are all taking a journey together, as parasocial as it may be, regardless of how well we know each other. Growth by fire. I also thank those who read the earlier online version and gave me feedback and anyone who has heard me rant and ramble about anything related to praxis and theology, in any context. You have helped to make this so, so much better, and I hope the changes have improved the work's accessibility, accuracy, and relevance to readers.

Outside of family and community, I have the authors of the books I have devoured over the course of my life to thank. Most of these books are long gone, decluttered when I down-sized to move to my current city. The items below are the best I have to offer by way of a reference list. I also added some footnote links in *The Soul's Inner Statues* itself — often to apps and pages. What is linked in footnotes or referenced below represent what was most on my mind while I was writing. The foundations and scaffolding of *The Soul's Inner Statues* came from blog posts published on KALLISTI and its predecessor (also named KALLISTI) between 2009 and 2022. Link rot is real, so if any of the links in either the Further Reading or Bibliography go somewhere else, please use the Internet Archive's Wayback Machine at https://archive.org.

Now, let's talk about the reference list. I have divided it into two sections: Items that are useful to consider as next-step reads and things that are cited. Citation is an acknowledgment of the influence of concepts and an important part of maintaining integrity, avoiding false speech, and refraining from plagiarism. Items in the "next-step reads" section are things that I consider generally useful for orienting yourself if you want to read anything more. Please apply discernment, though. I don't agree with everything that the people I mention say, but I think it's valuable to mull over a wide range of perspectives. There is no risk that reading people we disagree with will change our core beliefs. The only thing that can shift those is a self-shaking experience or upheaval, good or bad. What is most important is reflecting on what is said, who says it, and how it applies to your own practice, not uncritically following someone.[1]

10.2 Next-Step Reads

In library science, we do something called "reader's advisory" — a jargon term for connecting readers to books they want. The list below includes resources from the bibliography above that are useful for further reading for a newcomer, in addition to some things that I have *not* read that seem like they would

---

[1]The *New York Times* has a wonderful article about how to be a better reader, and it covers everything from reading what you disagree with to how to ask questions. https://www.nytimes.com/explain/2022/how-to-be-a-better-reader.

be a helpful next step for someone beginning a ritual practice. These include books, websites, and some video media. I tried to be expansive here. I admit that there is a "Western" bias to what *practical* materials are included, partly for ethical reasons when it comes to continuous traditions, where it is crucial to seek guidance and mentorship from people within the spiritual community to be in right relation with them. Moreover, in a global society, it is important to have solid information in hand to wayfind successfully. To that end, a few of the materials below are more about building multicultural awareness than they are about starting a specific practice. The bibliography after this section contains many more items — ones that I cited in *The Soul's Inner Statues* — and I encourage you to follow up on any of the ones of interest to you.

Addey, Tim. *The Unfolding Wings: The Way of Perfection in the Platonic Tradition*. Westbury: Prometheus Trust, 2011.

Bernstein, Frances. *Classical Living: A Month to Month Guide to Ancient Rituals for Heart and Home*. 1st edition. San Francisco: HarperOne, 2000.

Bettini, Maurizio. *In Praise of Polytheism*. Oakland, CA: University of California Press, 2023. Reprinted from the Italian edition from the Società editrice il Mulino, Bologna, 2014.

DuBois, Page. *A Million and One Gods: The Persistence of Polytheism*. Cambridge, MA: Harvard University Press, 2014.

Epstein, Nadine, and Rosita Arvigo. *Spiritual Bathing: Healing Rituals and Traditions from Around the World*. Reprint, Revised ed. Echo Point Books & Media, 2018.

Fuller, C. J. *The Camphor Flame: Popular Hinduism and Society in India – Revised and Expanded Edition*. Princeton, NJ: Princeton University Press, 2004.

Hegarty, Marissa. *An Introduction to Gaelic Polytheism*. Fith-Fath Publishing, 2022.

Heidi. "Smoke Cleansing Around the World." *Mountain Rose Herbs* (blog), July 26, 2021. https://blog.mountainroseher bs.com/smoke-cleansing

"Household Deity." In *Wikipedia*, July 9, 2022. https://en.wik ipedia.org/w/index.php?title=Household_deity&oldid =1097197400

Johnsen, Linda. *Lost Masters: Sages of Ancient Greece*. Honesdale, PA: Himalayan Institute Press, 2007.

Kirsch, Jonathan. *God Against The Gods: The History of the War Between Monotheism and Polytheism*. New York: Viking Compass, Penguin Group, 2004.

Mandell, Mindy. *Discovering the Beauty of Wisdom*. Prometheus Trust, 2020.

Mesteth, Wilmer Stampede, Darrell Standing Elk, and Phyllis Swift Hawk. "Declaration of War Against Exploiters of Lakota Spirituality." *Declaration made at Lakota Summit V*, 1993. `https://digitalhistory.uh.edu/disp_textbook.cfm?smtid=3&psid=730`

Ni, Xueting Christine. *From Kuan Yin to Chairman Mao: The Essential Guide to Chinese Deities*. Newburyport, MA: Weiser Books, 2018.

Nolan, Barbara. *A Year of Pagan Prayer: A Sourcebook of Poems, Hymns, and Invocations from Four Thousand Years of Pagan History*. Woodbury, Minnesota: Llewellyn Publications, 2021.

Nordvig, Mathias. *Ásatrú for Beginners: A Modern Heathen's Guide to the Ancient Northern Way*. Emeryville, CA: Rockridge Press, 2020.

Pennick, Nigel. *The Pagan Book of Days: A Guide to the Festivals, Traditions, and Sacred Days of the Year*. Revised edition. Rochester, VT: Destiny Books, 2001.

Raheem, Octavia F. *Pause, Rest, Be: Stillness Practices for Courage in Times of Change*. Boulder, Colorado: Shambhala, 2022.

Omland, Correne. *Smoke Cleansing: What It Is and How to Perform It*, 2021. `https://youtube.com/watch?v=_oFzD2ByB4o`

Panopoulos, Christos Pandion and Panagiotis Meton Pana-
giotopoulos. *Hellenic Polytheism: Household Worship*. Trans.
by Lesley Madytinou and Rathamanthys Madytinos. CreateS-
pace, 2014.

O'Brien, Suzanne Crawford and Inés Talamantez. *Religion and
Culture in Native America*. New York: Rowman & Littlefield,
2021.[2]

Olupona, Jacob K. *African Religions: A Very Short Introduction*.
New York: Oxford University Press, 2014.

Sengupta, Hindol. *Being Hindu: Understanding a Peaceful Path
in a Violent World*. Lanham: Rowman & Littlefield, 2018.

Solstice. *The Earth Spirit Hearth and Home: A Seasonal Guide
for a Nature-Based Home*. Grove City: Earth Spirit Press, 2022.

Temperance, Elani. "Khernips [Purification] Masterpost." *Bar-
ing the Aegis* (blog), May 2016. https://baringtheaegis.blo
gspot.com/2016/05/khernips-masterpost.html

Widugeni, Segomâros. *Ancient Fire: An Introduction to Gaulish
Celtic Polytheism*. Amelia, OH: ADF Publishing, 2018.

Wijeyakumar, Anusha. *Meditation with Intention: Quick & Easy*

---

[2]I decided to provide you with a recommendation for this book in addition to the "Declaration of War Against Exploiters of Lakota Spirituality" in
the hopes that both texts, when taken together, will help the reader be dis-
cerning — avoiding plastic shamans and disrespectful New Age practices.

Ways to Create Lasting Peace. Woodbury, Minnesota: Llewellyn Publications, 2021.

Bibliography

ACRL (Feb. 2015). *Framework for Information Literacy for Higher Education*. Text. Association of College & Research Libraries (ACRL). URL: https://www.ala.org/acrl/standards/il framework.

Addey, Tim (2000). *The Seven Myths of the Soul*. English. Westbury: Promethus Trust. ISBN: 978-1-898910-37-4.

— (2011). *The Unfolding Wings: The Way of Perfection in the Platonic Tradition*. Westbury. ISBN: 978-1-898910-94-7.

Anonymous (1994). *Anonymous Prolegomena to Platonic Philosophy*. Trans. by L. G. Westerink. Westbury: Prometheus Trust. ISBN: 978-1-898910-51-0.

— (n.d.). *The Orphic Hymns*. en. Trans. by Apostolos N. Athanassakis and Benjamin M. Wolkow. Johns Hopkins University Press. ISBN: 978-1-4214-0881-1. URL: https://www.press.jhu.edu/books/title/9661/orphic-hymns.

Apokatanidis, Katerina (Apr. 2021). *When Greece is not Ancient: Colonialism, Eurocentrism and Classics*. URL: https://everydayorientalism.wordpress.com/2021/04/27/when-greece-is-not-ancient-colonialism-eurocentrism-and-classics/.

Aristotle (2012). *Nicomachean Ethics.* University of Chicago Press. ISBN: 978-0-226-02675-6.

Avins, Jenni and Quartz (Oct. 2015). *The Dos and Don'ts of Cultural Appropriation.* URL: https://www.theatlantic.com/entertainment/archive/2015/10/the-dos-and-donts-of-cultural-appropriation/411292/.

Bryant, Edwin F. (2009). *Yoga Sutras of Patañjali.* New York: North Point Press. ISBN: 978-0-86547-736-0.

Butler, Edward P. (June 2016). "Polycentric Polytheism". en. In: *Witches & Pagans* 32, 37–40. URL: https://www.academia.edu/30296722/_Polycentric_Polytheism_pp_37_40_in_Witches_and_Pagans_32_June_2016_.

— (May 2019). *On Gods 'Behaving Badly'.* URL: https://endymions-bower.dreamwidth.org/57262.html.

— (2022). *The Way of the Gods: Polytheism(s) Around the World.* Notion Press.

Chart, David (2020). *Shinto Practice for Non-Japanese.* Vol. 5. Mimusubi Essays on Shinto. Mimusubi.

Clear, James (2018). *Atomic Habits: An Easy & Proven Way to Build Good Habits & Break Bad Ones.* Illustrated edition. New York: Avery. ISBN: 978-0-7352-1129-2.

Gaifman, Milette (2018). *The Art of Libation in Classical Athens.* Illustrated edition. New Haven Connecticut: Yale University Press. ISBN: 978-0-300-19227-8.

Griffin, Michael (Oct. 2020). *Michael Griffin, body and soul in Olympiodorus (Theandrites Conference 15 October 2020).* URL: https://www.youtube.com/watch?v=D8jl_NE47EY.

Harland, Philip A. (Mar. 2013). *Graffito for Apollo by the Boreikian Society (ca. 300 BCE).* URL: http://philipharland

.com/greco-roman-associations/dedication-to-bios
-life-by-the-boreikian-society-300-bce/.

Hermias (2018). *Hermias: On Plato Phaedrus 227A–245E*. Ed. by Richard Sorabji and Michael Griffin. Trans. by Michael Share and Dirk Baltzly. Ancient Commentators on Aristotle. Bloomsbury Academic. ISBN: 978-1-350-05188-1.

— (2022). *Hermias: On Plato Phaedrus 245E–257C*. English. Ed. by Richard Sorabji and Michael Griffin. Trans. by Michael Share and Dirk Baltzly. London ; New York: Bloomsbury Academic. ISBN: 978-1-350-05192-8.

Hoffner, Cynthia A. and Bradley J. Bond (June 2022). "Parasocial Relationships, Social Media, & Well-Being". In: *Current Opinion in Psychology* 45, 101306. ISSN: 2352-250X. DOI: 10.1016/j.copsyc.2022.101306.

Iamblichus (2003). *Iamblichus: On the Mysteries*. Trans. by Emma C. Clarke, John M. Dillon, and Jackson P. Hershbell. Bilingual edition. Atlanta: Society of Biblical Literature. ISBN: 978-1-58983-058-5.

— (2009). *Iamblichus of Chalcis: The Letters*. English. Trans. by John M. Dillon and Wolfgang Polleichtner. Atlanta: Society of Biblical Literature. ISBN: 978-1-58983-161-2.

— (2020). *Iamblichus' Life of Pythagoras, or Pythagoric Life Accompanied by Fragments of the Ethical Writings of Certain Pythagoreans in the Doric Dialect; and a Collection of Pythagoric Sentences from Stobaeus and Others, Which Are Omitted by Gale in His Opuscula Mythologica, and Have Not Been Noticed by Any Editor*. Trans. by Thomas Taylor. URL: https://www.gutenberg.org/ebooks/63300.

Jarzyna, Carol Laurent (Sept. 2021). "Parasocial Interaction, the COVID-19 Quarantine, and Digital Age Media". In: *Human Arenas* 4.3, 413–429. ISSN: 2522-5804. DOI: 10.1007/s 42087-020-00156-0.

Kornfield, Jack (2001). *After the Ecstasy, the Laundry: How the Heart Grows Wise on the Spiritual Path*. New York: Bantam.

Krasskova, Galina (Dec. 2017). *Public Service Announcement*. URL: https://krasskova.wordpress.com/2017/12/05/p ublic-service-announcement/.

Laërtius, Diogenes (1925). *Lives of the Eminent Philosophers*. Trans. by Robert Drew Hicks. URL: https://en.wikisour ce.org/wiki/Lives_of_the_Eminent_Philosophers.

Layne, Danielle A (2014). "The Character of Socrates and the Good of Dialogue Form: Neoplatonic Hermeneutics". In: *The Neoplatonic Socrates*. Ed. by Harold Tarrant and Danielle A Layne. University of Pennsylvania Press, 80–96.

— (Oct. 2017). "The Anonymous Prolegomena to Platonic Philosophy". In: *Brill's Companion to the Reception of Plato in Antiquity*, 533–554. DOI: 10.1163/9789004355385_031.

Majercik, Ruth (2013). *The Chaldean Oracles: Text, Translation and Commentary*. English. 2nd Edition. Prometheus Trust. ISBN: 978-1-898910-53-4.

Mandell, Mindy (2020). *Discovering the Beauty of Wisdom*. S.l.: Prometheus Trust. ISBN: 978-1-898910-72-5.

Meshi, Dar and Morgan E. Ellithorpe (Aug. 2021). "Problematic Social Media Use and Social Support Received in Real-Life versus on Social Media: Associations with Depression, Anxiety and Social Isolation". In: *Addictive Behaviors*

119, 106949. ISSN: 0306-4603. DOI: 10.1016/j.addbeh.202 1.106949.

Montell, Amanda (2021). *Cultish: The Language of Fanaticism*. English. New York, NY: Harper Wave. ISBN: 978-0-06-299315-1.

Moore, Meido (2020). *Hidden Zen: Practices for Sudden Awakening and Embodied Realization*. Boulder, Colorado: Shambhala. ISBN: 978-1-61180-846-9.

Nabarz, Payam (2009). *Stellar Magic: A Practical Guide to the Rites of the Moon, Planets, Stars and Constellations*. London: Avalonia. ISBN: 978-1-905297-25-2.

Nordvig, Mathias (2020). *Ásatrú for Beginners: A Modern Heathen's Guide to the Ancient Northern Way*. Emeryville, CA: Rockridge Press.

Nowakowski, David (n.d.). *Meditation – David Nowakowski*. en-US. URL: https://davidnowakowski.net/meditation/.

Olympiodorus (2015). *Olympiodorus : Life of Plato and On Plato First Alcibiades 1-9*. Ed. by Richard Sorabji and Michael Griffin. Trans. by Michael Griffin. Ancient Commentators on Aristotle. London: Bloomsbury Academic. ISBN: 978-1-4742-2028-6 978-1-4725-8830-2 978-1-4725-8832-6 978-1-4725-8831-9. DOI: 10.5040/9781474220286.

Parker, Robert (2017). *Greek Gods Abroad: Names, Natures, and Transformations*. English. Oakland, CA: University of California Press. ISBN: 978-0-52-029394-6.

Petrovic, Andrej and Ivana Petrovic (2016). *Inner Purity and Pollution in Greek Religion: Volume I: Early Greek Religion*. Oxford: Oxford University Press. ISBN: 978-0-19-876804-3. DOI: 10.1093/acprof:oso/9780198768043.001.0001.

Plato (1997). *Plato: Complete Works*. English. Ed. by John M. Cooper and D. S. Hutchinson. Indianapolis, Ind: Hackett Publishing Co. ISBN: 978-0-87220-349-5.

— (2016). *Plato: Laws*. Ed. by Malcolm Schofield. Trans. by Tom Griffith. New York: Cambridge University Press. ISBN: 978-0-521-67690-8.

Plotinus (2018). *Plotinus: The Enneads*. Ed. by Lloyd P. Gerson. Trans. by Lloyd P. Gerson et al. New York: Cambridge University Press. ISBN: 978-1-107-00177-0.

Proclus (1995). *The Theology of Plato*. Trans. by Thomas Taylor. Frome, Somerset, UK: Prometheus Trust. ISBN: 978-1-898910-07-7.

— (2003). *On the Existence of Evils*. Cornell University Press. ISBN: 978-0-8014-4100-4.

— (2007). *On Providence*. Trans. by Carlos G Steel. Ithaca, N.Y.: Cornell University Press. ISBN: 978-1-4725-5212-9.

— (2012). *Ten Problems Concerning Providence*. Trans. by Jan Opsomer and Carlos G Steel. London: Bristol Classical Press. ISBN: 978-1-4725-5214-3 978-0-7156-3924-5 978-1-4725-0095-3 978-1-4725-0178-3.

— (2013). *Commentary on Plato's Timaeus: Volume 5 - Book 4*. Trans. by Dirk Baltzly. Cambridge University Press.

— (2022). *Commentary on Plato's Republic*. en. Trans. by Dirk Baltzly, John F. Finamore, and Graeme Miles. Vol. 2. Cambridge University Press. ISBN: 978-1-107-15471-1. DOI: 10.1017/9781316650912.

Raheem, Octavia F. (2022). *Pause, Rest, Be: Stillness Practices for Courage in Times of Change*. Boulder, Colorado: Shambhala. ISBN: 978-1-61180-985-5.

Rowe, Christopher (Feb. 2015). "Methodologies for Reading
    Plato". In: *The Oxford Handbook of Topics in Philosophy*. Ox-
    ford University Press. DOI: 10.1093/oxfordhb/97801999
    35314.013.28.

Rugnetta, Mike and Kornhaber Brown (Nov. 2014). *Hell Is Quot-
    ing Other People | Idea Channel | PBS Digital Studios*. PBS Idea
    Channel. URL: https://www.youtube.com/watch?v=Jz
    YPUP6LR5Y.

Rumi, Jalaluddin (n.d.). *'The Guest House' by Jalaluddin Rumi*.
    URL: https://www.scottishpoetrylibrary.org.uk/poe
    m/guest-house/.

Sallust (1793). *Sallustius On the Gods and the World*. Trans. by
    Thomas Taylor. URL: https://en.wikisource.org/wiki
    /Sallust_On_the_Gods_and_the_World/Sallust_on_th
    e_Gods_and_the_World.

Simplicius (2014). *On Epictetus Handbook 27-53*. English. Ed.
    by Richard Sorabji. Trans. by Charles Brittain and Tad
    Brennan. Ancient Commentators on Aristotle. London:
    Bloomsbury Academic. ISBN: 978-1-4725-5736-0.

Syrianus (2007). *On Aristotle Metaphysics 13-14*. Ed. by Richard
    Sorabji. Trans. by John Dillon. London: Bristol Classical
    Press. ISBN: 978-0-7156-3574-2.

Upadhyaya, Nidhi (Oct. 2021). *Young Hindus Get Creative with
    Home Temples in Cramped Apartments*. URL: https://reli
    gionnews.com/2021/10/13/millennial-hindus-get-cr
    eative-with-home-temples-in-cramped-apartments/.

Valkenburg, Patti M. (June 2022). "Social Media Use and Well-
    Being: What We Know and What We Need to Know". In:

Current Opinion in Psychology 45, 101294. ISSN: 2352-250X. DOI: 10.1016/j.copsyc.2021.12.006.

Wijeyakumar, Anusha (2021). *Meditation with Intention: Quick & Easy Ways to Create Lasting Peace*. Woodbury, Minnesota: Llewellyn Publications. ISBN: 978-0-7387-6268-5.

Wikipedia contributors (July 2022). *Household Deity*. URL: https://en.wikipedia.org/w/index.php?title=Household_deity%5C&oldid=1097197400.

Wildermuth, Rhyd (June 2021). *A Plague of Gods: Cultural Appropriation and the Resurgent Left Sacred*. URL: abeautifulresistance.org/site/2021/6/03/plague-of-gods.